the

reclaiming the lost art of romance

old fashioned ♡ way

GINGER KOLBABA

based on the screenplay by rik swartzwelder

Tyndale House Publishers, Inc.
Carol Stream, Illinois

Visit Tyndale online at www.tyndale.com.

TYNDALE and Tyndale's quill logo are registered trademarks of Tyndale House Publishers, Inc.

The Old Fashioned Way: Reclaiming the Lost Art of Romance

Copyright © 2014 by Old is New, LLC. All rights reserved.

Cover photograph of leather copyright © Spiderplay/iStockphoto. All rights reserved.

Designed by Jacqueline L. Nuñez

Edited by Jonathan Schindler

Exclusive representation by Working Title Agency, LLC, Spring Hill, TN. Published in association with Books and Such, Inc., Attn: Janet Kobobel Grant, 5926 Sunhawk Dr., Santa Rosa, CA 95409.

Unless otherwise indicated, all Scripture quotations are taken from the *Holy Bible*, New Living Translation, second edition, copyright © 1996, 2004, 2007 by Tyndale House Foundation. (Some quotations may be from the NLT, first edition, copyright © 1996.) Used by permission of Tyndale House Publishers, Inc., Carol Stream, Illinois 60188. All rights reserved.

Scripture quotations marked KJV are taken from the *Holy Bible*, King James Version.

Scripture quotations marked *The Message* are taken from *The Message* by Eugene H. Peterson, copyright © 1993, 1994, 1995, 1996, 2000, 2001, 2002. Used by permission of NavPress Publishing Group. All rights reserved.

Scripture quotations marked NASB are taken from the New American Standard Bible,® copyright © 1960, 1962, 1963, 1968, 1971, 1972, 1973, 1975, 1977, 1995 by The Lockman Foundation. Used by permission.

Scripture quotations marked NIV are taken from the Holy Bible, *New International Version*,® *NIV*.® Copyright © 1973, 1978, 1984, 2011 by Biblica, Inc.™ Used by permission of Zondervan. All rights reserved worldwide. www.zondervan.com.

Library of Congress Cataloging-in-Publication Data

Kolbaba, Ginger.
    The old fashioned way : reclaiming the lost art of romance / Ginger Kolbaba.
        pages cm
    "Based on the screenplay by Rik Swartzwelder."
    Includes bibliographical references.
    ISBN 978-1-4143-7974-6 (sc)
1. Man-woman relationships—Religious aspects—Christianity. 2. Love—Religious aspects—Christianity. 3. Dating (Social custom)—Religious aspects—Christianity. I. Title.
    BT705.8.K66 2013
    248.8'4—dc23   2013009928

Printed in the United States of America

20   19   18   17   16   15   14

7   6   5   4   3   2   1

table of contents

a note from rik swartzwelder

When you are a writer, you are often asked the question, "How did you come up with the idea for fill-in-the-blank?"

In the case of *Old Fashioned*, this question is hard to answer. As Clay says in the film, "It wasn't just one thing; it was more like a lot of little things, all adding up."

If I *had* to pick a starting point, it would be that I'd begun to feel the absence of a movie that accurately reflected the lives of the people I knew personally: single people who took the idea of honoring God in their dating relationships seriously. *How would a movie like that look?* I wondered. *And how could you craft it in a way that wasn't propaganda or completely Pollyanna?*

A lot of other stuff went into the mix, of course, but that was the start. As I sketched out the basic outline of the story, I knew I needed an image that would be a cornerstone for the film. Such things do not always come easy in the creative process, but this time I saw it right away.

Feet at a threshold.

I couldn't shake that image or the idea that most mistakes in life are cemented by choices made long before any actual "fall." We cross a threshold, and that leads to . . . and that leads to . . .

What if you applied that image to a romantic context, and what if you had a character who took that threshold seriously—a character who, for whatever reason, had committed himself to make decisions in advance of the moment? Maybe he began living this way for redemptive reasons, maybe it morphs into a form of isolation that he never intended, maybe he begins to doubt.

What if?

That was the birth of the rather odd and curious character of Clay Walsh and the genesis of what would eventually become the screenplay and motion picture titled *Old Fashioned*.

Cut! Print! Moving on! But why *this* book?

Good question. I can assure you that when I first sat down to write the screenplay for *Old Fashioned*, the last thing on my mind was a nonfiction companion book about dating, courtship, and romance.

I would never claim to be any kind of expert on those things. (I can supply much expert testimony and many witnesses confirming that I am not.) And second, more important, movies are about story above all. About entertainment. True, good movies can be more. They can educate, they can inspire, they can nudge the world in a new and positive direction. But unless they entertain, none of those more noble aspirations has a chance.

We don't go to the movies to see a "how to" on any given topic; we go to be transported outside of ourselves, to share in and somehow connect with the journey of another. To be moved. How-to manuals, no matter how helpful they are, rarely move us in the same way that a film or a song or a painting can.

In saying that, I don't mean to slight how-to books at all; they are needed. Generally speaking, books are much better suited to reflection, to stopping and starting, to digging deeper into an idea and looking at it from all angles and challenging the assumptions and premises of any given work or presentation. And, curiously, our primary purpose when reading a book like this one usually is *not* entertainment. We read it because we want to learn, we want to drill down, we want to grow. In a sense, we are already invested, at least at some level, in the message of the book.

This isn't to say that movies don't have messages. They do. All of them. There's a famous quote (usually attributed to Samuel Goldwyn) that goes, "If you want to send a message, call Western Union." But as Gary Cooper says in *Meet John Doe*, "That's a lotta hooey!"

Every movie has a message. From *Schindler's List* to *The Hangover*, all movies are saying something—usually lots of things, whether intended or not. People usually only refer to that Goldwyn quote when they have a preexisting strong disagreement with any perceived "message."

That said, where I think Goldwyn was 100 percent right was that if you want to give a sermon, you should give a sermon, not shoehorn it into celluloid (or pixels) and pretend it's a movie.

My creative team and I thought about that quite a bit while making *Old Fashioned*. We worked hard to make the "messages" in our movie organic to the characters and the situations. We consciously tried to keep our movie from becoming a how-to manual or a testament to those blessed few who have made all the right choices. Our characters make mistakes: they are flawed, they are human. Now, whether we succeeded in our storytelling goals is for audiences and critics to decide.

But regardless of how the prevailing winds of popular opinion blow, one thing is fairly clear: *Old Fashioned* raises more questions than it answers. Personally, I like movies that do that. It's somehow disingenuous to have a two-hour monologue that doesn't give voice to opposition or that wraps everything up perfectly. In some ways, I think our film serves primarily as the *beginning* of a conversation, a dialogue.

So I saw this book as an opportunity to continue the conversation in a way that our movie never could (or should, really). After many hours of thoughtful and genuine conversation, I can say with confidence that Ginger Kolbaba and the team at Tyndale have captured the vision of *Old Fashioned* and illuminated its message in a way that will encourage, strengthen, and challenge you wherever you are in your romantic life.

The times we live in can be difficult and uncertain, particularly for singles, and we need a sane approach to relationships that affirms the reality of human nature and our need for divine intervention. This book will help you take an honest look both at your relationships and at some of the traditions that through the years have been carelessly tossed aside.

Thank you so much for sharing in this conversation with us. May you be as blessed as we have been by the experience.

when life was simpler: welcome to the old fashioned way

"There's got to be a better way," a friend told me recently. We'd been chatting about her latest dates, in which she felt pressured and confused and completely unsatisfied. "Why can't we go back to the way things used to be?"

"What do you mean?" I asked, sensing I already knew the answer.

"You know, when life was simpler. Men were, well . . ." She paused, as if embarrassed about what she was thinking.

"Men?" I offered. "A time when we knew our roles? And when that wasn't a bad thing? When we knew what to expect from each other?"

"Yes!" She pointed at me emphatically. "That's it exactly. It's like nobody knows how to date anymore, or even really how to have a committed relationship. You go out, then the next thing you know, you're sleeping together with no commitment and no plans to get married." She sighed. "I know this isn't what God has in mind, but I don't know what to do about it."

My friend isn't the only one feeling that way. I know lots of singles—women and men—who are wandering around the dating circuit confused, unsure, and unhappy about relationships.

They are looking for a better way, a simpler way. A more satisfying and God-honoring way.

Maybe they are looking for the old fashioned way. Maybe you are too.

Old fashioned. What images come to mind when you hear that phrase?

If it's old fashioned cooking with meat loaf and gravy, homemade biscuits, and pink lemonade, followed by a generous helping of churned butter-pecan ice cream, you may smile and think, *I sure could use some of* that *old fashioned.* Or maybe it's porch swings, rowboats, clothes hanging on the line, Aunt Bee, and Mayberry. And it fills you with a sense of joy and longing.

But what if you think of old fashioned clothes—those constrictive, high collars, two hundred buttons, and layers upon layers? You probably aren't smiling now. Not to mention, weren't those also the days when glimpsing a woman's ankle could cause a man to have a strong hankering after sinful things? Or maybe you think of old fashioned as the patriarchal, sexist, chauvinistic, we-like-our-women-barefoot-and-pregnant baloney.

Often when we think about *old fashioned,* we think in extremes: the yummy, high-fat, high-calorie, oh-those-were-the-days delights or the tighter-than-tight, no-grace, prudish, yowsa-*those*-were-the-days angst.

But what about old fashioned romance? What if living (or loving) the old fashioned way wasn't as bad as you may at first think? What if it actually helped you find peace and satisfaction? Is it possible that we've put old fashioned courtship and romance into the same category as the high-collared, puritanical outfits? That we've pushed them off without considering the many joys and possibilities they offer for real, authentic, and deep relationships?

Old fashioned can be a provocative and divisive label, no question. And I certainly don't intend to imply that life in generations past was perfect. After all, the writer of Ecclesiastes reminds us not to "long for 'the good old days,' for you don't know whether they were any better than today" (7:10). We know that things in "the good old days" weren't always as they seemed. People in the past weren't necessarily paragons of purity who consistently fought sexual urges. While certain behaviors may have become more "open" in recent years (say, after the sexual revolution of the 1960s), that doesn't mean those behaviors are new. Grandma Johnson used to say, "Kids today are just doing on the front porch what we used to do on the back porch."

So we know "the good old days" had their issues, but perhaps there *are* some things we've left behind that are worth reconsidering for the way we handle our relationships.

In the following pages you'll read forty days' worth of ideals and thoughts that may seem strange, foreign, or possibly downright hokey. You may agree with some and turn up your nose at others. You may think, *Yeah, well, sure it worked for couples in the past, but that's so . . . yesterday.* And that's okay. My goal isn't to twist your arm. But I hope that you'll at least give these ideals some genuine, open-minded, and honest consideration—that you'll pray about them and see how God leads you.

This book isn't a compatibility workbook or a how-to-date manual, nor is it a book to act as a club to beat anyone up with. The goal isn't to lift up the people who have done it perfectly or to heap shame on those who have made bad choices.

Please remember, we've *all* made mistakes. The Christian life is a learning process. We all come from a place of brokenness, and we all long for a better world. The goal, the noble end, is the same for all of us: moving closer to God, closer to how we're called to live. The goal of this book is to inspire and create a hope and longing for us to be our best selves, regardless of how fractured we are.

If you've been hurt, or even if you have hurt others, that doesn't exclude you from the capacity to love and be loved. There is hope, and there *is* a better way.

Ultimately, this book is about grace—what we offer and what we can receive. The old fashioned way starts with how we treat others—before we even begin with romance. After all, we can't treat people badly in one area of our lives and expect to behave better in romance. Who we are and how we treat others will inevitably seep into our romantic relationships.

Living the old fashioned way means being intentional in our relationships. It thinks in terms of *I* and *Thou* (such a great and little-used word nowadays!), always considering others above ourselves (you can read more about "I" and "Thou" relationships on Days 6 and 10). The focus is on the other person—which is the essence of the Golden Rule ("Do to others whatever you would like them to do to you"—Matthew 7:12).

So let's take this journey and explore these ideas together. Let's look at the ways and traditions of the past. Not with rose-colored glasses that deny what was destructive. But let's examine the good things in the past that were in place to protect us—things like courtship (taking dating and relationships slowly and thoughtfully), chaperones (today's equivalent of getting your friends and family involved in your dating life and listening to their wisdom), and modesty (respecting ourselves and the way we present ourselves to others).

This book came about from several conversations with Rik Swartzwelder, the screenwriter and director of the movie *Old Fashioned*, as well as from the movie and the novel based on it.* Both that movie and this book attempt to challenge our modern way of looking at romantic relationships with wisdom from the past. If you're just beginning your romantic journey, this book may help you avoid some pitfalls. And even if this is round two, ten, or twenty for you, your life can blossom far beyond whatever damage has been done to you or that you may have done to others. The rest of your life doesn't have to be what it was. It can be better; it can be beautiful. The old fashioned way: let's find it.

---

*For a plot summary and additional information about *Old Fashioned* (the movie and the book), turn to page 221.

what's right about today's dating scene

CLAY: I don't believe our job is the looking, it's the becoming. Once we are the right person . . . when we're ready . . .
AMBER: But if you don't ever date, how will you know?
—OLD FASHIONED

MY FRIEND TODD HAS BEEN MARRIED FIVE YEARS. He and his wife have built a strong relationship that has carried them through job loss and several other challenges. They've started a family, and whenever I talk with him or hear updates on him from other friends, the news is always good. He's happy. He's satisfied. He's still deeply in love.

Todd and his wife met through an online dating service.

Wait, an online dating service? How is that old fashioned?

After Todd spent years searching for the right woman, going on numerous dates—some he initiated, others initiated for him through the infamous blind-date system—he felt more and more discouraged at his prospects.

"Nothing felt right," he says. "I wasn't dating anyone, was scarred by past hurt, and felt pretty lonely. I began wrestling with why it seemed that every woman I met was not a right fit—it was always a dance of square pegs and round holes. *Maybe*, I thought, *the selective matching of online dating would present not just a wider pool—but prescreened compatibility.*"[1]

That it did. And after a month of talking over the computer and phone and learning more about each other's character, likes, dislikes, temperaments, and personalities, Todd and his now-wife decided to meet each other. They had a good foundation to start building a relationship on. And the rest, as they say, is history.

Technology, the improvement of life, and our contemporary dating scene have a lot of great things going on. Some Internet dating sites—such as eHarmony—have hit upon an important aspect of building the basics of relationships. Rather than focusing on physical attributes and sexual chemistry as the main determinants of relational worthiness, these sites center on personality and character, understanding that marriage needs more than physical attraction to make it last.

Modern dating also allows people to focus on building friendships. I know many couples who date in group settings, for instance, in order to allow their trusted friends and family to help them see their potential beloved in a more objective light. Singles groups, church groups, and hobby groups allow for interaction and connection in a (hopefully!) nonthreatening way.

To be sure, nothing is perfect in the world of dating, so you may have tried these options and found them lacking.

Where Todd and his wife got it right was in not idealizing romance. The good thing that many online dating services have going for them is that they push their users to address things that may never get out in the open in a dating relationship: who the other person really is—not the facade he or she is presenting, the issues that are important, deal makers and breakers. Dating websites and similar opportunities allow the user to bring these issues to the forefront so that prospective dates can get a quicker understanding of what makes a person tick—issues that may not come out in a relationship until further down the road or even never at all—until meeting the divorce attorney after a marriage has gone sour.

I am not implying that today's dating scene or Internet dating sites or church singles groups are holy ground, nor am I suggesting that you sign up for an online dating service. I just wanted you to know that even though I'm advocating the old fashioned way, today's dating scene has some old fashioned similarities that are worth considering and affirming: namely, getting to know the other person beyond appearance and physical chemistry.

If you live a life guided by wisdom, you won't limp or stumble as you run.
—PROVERBS 4:12

JOURNAL

- List some of the good aspects of today's dating ideas and methods. Then explain why you think they are good. For instance, if you list personality compatibility profiles, offer reasons for needing to know about someone's personality before you get too involved in a relationship or why the other person needs to know about your personality.
- Think about what you can offer another person. What are your strengths, not just in a romantic way, but in a lifelong-partner way? What are some weaknesses that you need to work on? Write those out, and then discuss them with God.

PRAYER

God, I've gone in so many different directions, trying to find the right person I can share my life with. I'm often discouraged and frustrated because no one seems to fit or truly connect with me. I've made a lot of mistakes along the way.

Help me to see beyond the typical dating scene and look to the type of person who can grow my character and love me for who I am, and whom I can love as you love. But most of all, keep me attuned to your desires for whom I should allow into my life in a deeper, more committed way.

what's right about yesteryear's dating scene

I know how weird it sounds . . . but a lot of the boundaries that used to be common, that we've thrown away, were there to protect us. We don't have to go around using each other, hurting each other. It doesn't have to be that way.

—CLAY, *OLD FASHIONED*

I REMEMBER WHEN I FOUND OUT my friend Amanda (not her real name) was moving in with her boyfriend of two months—a man who had a string of ex-girlfriends (with whom he had also fathered children). In fact, he was still living with his most recent ex-girlfriend and their baby and was now dating my friend.

"Amanda, why would you do that?" I asked. "He's still involved with his ex!"

"Well, not really," she told me matter-of-factly. "He's still living there, but that's it."

She informed me that they were moving in together because it would be cheaper, plus it would help them know better if they were compatible enough to get married.

I pulled out every reason I could think of for them not to move their relationship in the direction they were headed. I told her that statistically speaking, couples who live together before they marry are more likely to get divorced and to experience domestic violence, and they actually experience less satisfaction in their marriages than if they wait to live together until after they marry.[1] I told her that as Christians we are called to live differently—counterculturally—from what the world says is acceptable, that God's boundaries were put in place for healthy, good reasons.

Her response: "I don't set myself up for failure."

Life in the "good old days" seems passé and prudish. Our culture tells us that if we love someone, we should be able to be with that person immediately and experience all the benefits of married life without actually being married. Our culture continues to try to eliminate sexual behavior from discussions of morality.

To a crowd of civil-rights activists in the black American community, comedian Bill Cosby recently said, "No longer is a person embarrassed because they're pregnant without a husband. No longer is a boy considered an embarrassment if he tries to run away from being [a] father."[2]

Although Cosby's comments drew criticism, he makes a good point. Yesteryear's way of dating and commitment in relationships may have been more difficult, but it was ultimately set up to protect us from undue harm and shame. It kept our consciences and actions in check. Part of being old fashioned is having a realistic view of sin, the world, and human nature. To be sure, the church throughout the years has in many ways overcompensated on the shame part, but being truly old fashioned is a balance of understanding sin and forgiveness, shame and grace.

Abolishing shame completely signifies how much we've lost the moral compass that God designed for us and that society, for so long, held us accountable to.

Instead, today men who try to act chivalrous are often accused of being sexist. We talk about "friends with benefits" as though we can separate the physical actions from the emotional, spiritual, and psychological consequences. Old cultural norms and assumptions are not necessarily true: men *and* women are now both "players." And without beating up too much on Hollywood or pop culture, many would acknowledge that we send a confusing message to ourselves and to the rest of the world.

Going back to the traditions of our past isn't a bad thing! Although they are counter to what our culture (and even some churches now, sadly) says is "normal," they also safeguard our hearts, minds, and bodies from regret and hurt. These traditions keep us pure (an old fashioned word!) and protected for the person who will ultimately become our spouse.

But you may be thinking, *Well, I've blown it. I'm not "pure."* The beauty of this ideal is that through forgiveness, God can clean up your past and make you pure again. Purity really isn't just a one-time cleansing and then you're done; it is ongoing. And thankfully, God offers us a better way to live and relate to others—and with that comes a clear conscience and, ultimately, peace.

Those who are dominated by the sinful nature think about sinful things, but those who are controlled by the Holy Spirit think about things that please the Spirit. So letting your sinful nature control your mind leads to death. But letting the Spirit control your mind leads to life and peace.

—ROMANS 8:5-6

CONSIDER THIS

- What are some things current cultural attitudes would believe are old fashioned in relationships? Do you believe those things are old fashioned? Why or why not?

- If you've struggled with living out old fashioned ideals, has it been because of pressure from others? Some other reason? How were you swayed?

JOURNAL

The apostle Paul offers one of the best yeses in the Bible. Read Romans 8:5-6 (today's Scripture verse) and consider: Is this true in your life? Think about the times in your life and your relationships when you said yes to God's Spirit leading you. Did that decision give you peace? Write about those times as reminders of the power and importance of saying yes to the right things.

Now think about the times in your life and your relationships when you went your own way, pressured someone to cave in, or caved in yourself to the pressure of others around you. How did those decisions make you feel? Did they provide peace, or regret and angst? Write about those times as reminders of the importance of staying true to God's call for morality on your life.

but the old fashioned way is so *old fashioned*

There are no knights in shining armor, but you think you're Cinderella, don't you?

—LUCKY CHUCKY, *OLD FASHIONED*

IN *OLD FASHIONED* THE CHARACTER LUCKY CHUCKY is a radio shock jock who doesn't agree with pursuing an old fashioned way of life. He believes that life is meant to be enjoyed without bounds. He sees the hypocritical nature of people who say one thing and act differently. He observes that those in the church often seem as lost and confused on this stuff as "the world" is, that chivalry is dead, monogamy is outdated, and abstinence is for, well, no one. If you feel it, do it. Don't allow the emotional or spiritual side to get tangled up in the mess. Relationships are first and foremost about chemistry, he believes. Or simply personal pleasure.

Apart from any spiritual or religious boundaries, let's be honest: what Lucky Chucky believes makes sense. The physical side of romance feels good. Why not enjoy it without the strings of commitment and responsibility? Besides, as the cliché goes, everyone else is doing it.

But when we throw out the sacred traditions of the past, we lose something in the process. "You can tell a lot about a society by who it chooses to celebrate," a TV reporter says in Woody Allen's film *Celebrity*. I think the reporter is right. The traditions of the past encouraged us to love and respect our neighbors, to offer kindness and service to others in need. We once praised Neil Armstrong, police officers, and Mother Teresa. Now we can't get our fill of *Jersey Shore*, TMZ, and *Glamour* magazine.

Aside from his cynical view of love and relationships, there's some truth in what Lucky Chucky says. It isn't pleasant, but his assessment of a lot of things is dead on. He sees the superficiality of contemporary love for what it is and doesn't pretend that it's anything other than what it is on the surface. He says, "Women are just like men; everyone wants it both ways." In other words, a woman might want the rebel, the "bad boy," but she also wants someone who is faithful. We might be drawn to someone for all the wrong reasons, so we shouldn't act brokenhearted when that person behaves as we might expect him or her (this goes both ways) to behave.

This is true even in church. I see young, quiet, sincere guys who are trying desperately to live authentic, God-honoring lives and beautiful, young, Christian girls who say that's what they want. But then the girls pursue someone who has more charisma and maybe has been blessed with more social skills but may or may not be pursuing God with his whole heart. Obviously, I'm oversimplifying here, but imagine the Christian guy who's trying to live a godly life, but at church all the girls are talking about how awesome Channing Tatum (or fill in the blank with some hunky movie star) is. Every time I'm in a situation where I hear that, it breaks my heart. The women aren't saying that Channing Tatum (or celeb of the month) is awesome because he's pursuing God in his life. They're saying he's awesome because he's got a great body and he's handsome and charismatic. And that's it. It has nothing to do with his values, his level of integrity, or anything that matters at all.

Part of the reason old fashioned values can seem so old fashioned to us is that we've bought into the world's way of viewing relationships. What we say we want and what we actually want are often different things, and so we become confused as to what it means to follow God in our romantic relationships.

As we consider pursuing the old fashioned way, may the blatant honesty of Lucky Chucky remind us of the truth of who we are and who we don't have to be.

Since God chose you to be the holy people whom he loves, you must clothe yourselves with tenderhearted mercy, kindness, humility, gentleness, and patience.
—COLOSSIANS 3:12

CONSIDER THIS

- Read back over some of Lucky Chucky's attitudes I mentioned. Do any of those ring true in your actions, thoughts, or relationships?
- If they are true, why do you think that is? What do you think needs to happen in order to change that thought pattern or behavior?

PRAYER

God, I don't like the things that Lucky Chucky and people like him recognize and say. But some of those things are true about me. Point those things out to me when I'm tempted to go that way. Give me wisdom and discernment to see that attitude or behavior and then give me the strength to walk away from it and toward attitudes and behaviors that please you and honor those around me.

but i've done everything right!

I'd like to wring your neck. Look at you. The high and mighty. You expect the whole world to stand up and . . . do the wave for you, give you a trophy for being good.

—AUNT ZELLA TO CLAY, *OLD FASHIONED*

POOR CLAY. He works so hard at being good. He is trying to be a strong, dependable, noble man. Where he gets into trouble is he focuses so much on the letter of the law that he forgets the spirit of the law, the reason it's there in the first place. And that works itself out as self-righteousness, which can be a dangerous thing.

The letter of the law demands that we follow a strict set of rules: do not lie, do not commit adultery, do not, do not, do not . . .

The spirit of the law says the law is first and foremost about getting our hearts in the right place. It's about character and our relationship with God. Once we get our hearts in the right place, we will live according to the law not because we have to or out of fear that God will punish us, but rather because we want to please God and honor ourselves and others. We begin to understand the reasons behind the law, what God has done for us, and why he has set up certain boundaries for our good.

It takes Clay a long time to come to that realization in *Old Fashioned*. But in the midst of living such a rigid life, not only does pride set in (which is a sin, by the way), but also everything becomes about him (self-absorption—also a sin[1]). Aunt Zella says it this way: "If you were any more self-absorbed, you'd be a dot."

The apostle Paul puts it this way: "Don't think you are better than you really are. Be honest in your evaluation of yourselves, measuring yourselves by the faith God has given us" (Romans 12:3).

I hate to sound harsh here, but if you have avoided (or overcome) the obvious physical romantic sins, be careful of pride. It can infiltrate our attitudes and behaviors—even toward God. We can come off as though we're better than other people—especially if we feel they've fallen and we haven't. But we can also begin to feel that we deserve something from God or that God owes us the perfect romantic story because of our personal righteousness. Danger ahead!

You can take pride in the fact that you're still a virgin, for instance, but that doesn't mean you're immune to being self-centered or toying with people. Some of the most judgmental, merciless people I've ever met were also, technically at least, the "purest." They were virgins, but they also were incredible gossips or passive-aggressive manipulators or [you fill in the blank]. Few things are less attractive than a self-righteous virgin. We long for purity, but we long for humility, too. They go hand in hand.

The book of Proverbs speaks strongly against the sin of pride. Just look at these verses:

- "Pride leads to disgrace, but with humility comes wisdom." (Proverbs 11:2)
- "Pride goes before destruction, and haughtiness before a fall." (Proverbs 16:18)
- "Pride ends in humiliation, while humility brings honor." (Proverbs 29:23).

Jesus weighs in on the topic of pride. He told a parable "to some who had great confidence in their own righteousness and scorned everyone else":

> Two men went to the Temple to pray. One was a Pharisee, and the other was a despised tax collector. The Pharisee stood by himself and prayed this prayer: "I thank you, God, that I am not a sinner like everyone else. For I don't cheat, I don't sin, and I don't commit adultery. I'm certainly not like that tax collector! I fast twice a week, and I give you a tenth of my income."
>
> But the tax collector stood at a distance and dared not even lift his eyes to heaven as he prayed. Instead, he beat his chest in sorrow, saying, "O God, be merciful to me, for I am a sinner." I tell you, this sinner, not the Pharisee, returned home justified before God. For those who exalt themselves will be humbled, and those who humble themselves will be exalted. (Luke 18:9-14)

There are dangers to seeing ourselves as better than others or judging ourselves by spiritual success in a single area. The measure of our walk with God is not defined by any one thing alone. The ultimate measure of our spiritual maturity is to love and forgive others (and ourselves) as Christ loves and forgives us.

Not everyone's story or journey is the same. And a seemingly perfect track record in the romantic arena doesn't guarantee a "happily ever after." I know people who have done everything "right"— they've saved sex for marriage, for instance—and they've still ended up divorced or abandoned (through no fault of their own).

The heart of the old fashioned way is gratitude for life, grace, and the gifts God has given. Thank God for grace. Grace and law need each other; they balance each other out. "Unfailing love and truth have met together. Righteousness and peace have kissed!" writes the psalmist (Psalm 85:10).

Rather than falling victim to smugness, delight in redemptive love—something all of us need. And thankfully, God provides. How amazing that the highest form of Christlikeness takes us from being our own personal righteousness (thinking we can attain righteousness through our acts and will alone) to understanding we cannot. We fall on God's mercy—and then (and this is the incredible part) within us grows the ability to forgive others (and ourselves) the way that Christ forgives us.

So if you've done everything to the letter of the law, move forward in the grace and spirit of the law, offering grace to others who are on their own journeys. And if you've messed up royally and have crashed through the law, fall on God's grace. He never tires of our asking for forgiveness. He never turns away from a humble and contrite spirit. Never.

The high and lofty one who lives in eternity, the Holy One, says this: "I live in the high and holy place with those whose spirits are contrite and humble. I restore the crushed spirit of the humble and revive the courage of those with repentant hearts."

—ISAIAH 57:15

PRAYER

God, I've lived under the law for a long time and I've done it with wrong motives. Forgive me for trying to live by a strict set of rules without understanding your love and the reasons behind the rules. Help me to embrace the spirit of the law and to live humbly, forgiving others and myself. Help me to honor you in everything I do. And help me to bask in the amazing grace and forgiveness you offer.

CONSIDER THIS

- King David wrote Psalm 51 after the prophet Nathan confronted him about committing adultery with Bathsheba. Realizing what he'd done, he wrote, "My sacrifice, O God, is a broken spirit; a broken and contrite heart you, God, will not despise" (Psalm 51:17, NIV). If God forgave David of his sin, do you believe he can and will forgive you of yours?
- In what ways have you felt tempted to live with pride? How has that affected your interactions with and feelings toward others? Toward yourself?

longing for more

It seems to me we can never give up longing and wishing while we are thoroughly alive. There are certain things we feel to be beautiful and good, and we must hunger after them.

—GEORGE ELIOT

RELATIONSHIPS ARE COMPLICATED. From the moment God created Adam and Eve, humans have had a deep desire to know and be known. Our families know us; our friends know us. But they don't "complete" us, as Jerry Maguire so famously says in the movie of the same name.

We long for someone to connect with us, understand us, accept us. Forgive the seventies music kickback, but as Andy Gibb so eloquently sang, we want someone to tell us (or even sing to us!), "I just want to be your everything." We long for that, because that's the way God designed us. He created within us a desire for an intimate relationship—that two become one (see Genesis 2:24). But he also created us, ultimately, for more.

Sometimes in our quest to fulfill that God-given longing, we rush the process. We may put blinders on, date the wrong people, or get too physical or too emotionally attached too quickly. We may hide our true selves to find the "perfect" person or smother him or her with our neediness. We may place too great a burden on the other person to be our everything. How often we confuse "You complete me" with "You are the answer to my every need, want, desire: you will guarantee that I will never be lonely, unhappy, irritable, unhealthy, financially insecure, broken, hurt, or damaged."

The reality is that while God created us for community and authentic relationships, no person will be able to truly complete us. Because ultimately only God does. We have needs only God can satisfy. Although another person can satisfy some of them, only God can satisfy all of them, all the time.

Feeling lonely? God can help you. He is faithful.

Feeling unloved or unlovable? God can help you. He is faithful.

Feeling unacceptable? God can help you. He is faithful.

Having needs and expectations isn't bad. But where we set our hopes of fulfilling them will determine the success of having them met. When we look to another person to fulfill all our needs and wants, we limit that person's ability to bring strength and joy into the relationship. The strengths the other person brings actually get compromised by the expectations we've placed on him or her, which means we won't get the full benefit of what that person does bring. Or there's also the disastrous potential that if we try to be someone's everything, he or she may foolishly put us on a pedestal. So if instead of going to God and allowing him to complete us, we take those needs to another person, we can end up depleting that person, and then we end up denying ourselves the fullness of what he or she can really offer. As a result, we are all unable to live up to our potential in the relationship.

We need to ask ourselves: Do we even really love this person? Do we care about him or her, or are we motivated more by what the other person provides for us? It's important to pay attention and live with intention in our relationships, not simply to focus on how someone makes us feel.

Only when we enter a relationship with a healthy understanding of who we are as individuals and who we are in Christ will we be able to bring the best of ourselves to the relationship, *and only then* can we bring the best out of the other person.

This requires an honest look deep within our heart and an acknowledgment—maybe even for the first time!—that we can't do life well on our own and that we can't expect someone else to become our everything (even though Jerry Maguire's statement *is* a wonderfully romantic notion).

If you're serious about wanting to do life, relationships, and romance a different way, then it's time to square things up with God—who is full of mercy and compassion and is waiting to truly complete you and fulfill your needs. While a close relationship with another person can definitely enhance God's work in you, only God can completely, thoroughly satisfy you. Everyone and everything else will eventually let you down. God won't. (If the idea of "squaring things up with God" is new to you, check out Days 39 and 40 for more information on what that looks like.)

As you begin to pursue living the old fashioned way, it's important to understand that God is on your side, he is for you, and he wants to see you grow and live in deep and abundant joy. But more important than your finding a mate, God is concerned about your relationship with him and growing you into the person he has created *you* to be. When you accept and pursue that spiritual relationship, then you'll find yourself more satisfied with your life and circumstances in general and less in need of someone else to be responsible for who you are and what you need. And you'll be ready and better able to love someone romantically, if and when that time comes.

You know what I long for, Lord; you hear my every sigh.

—PSALM 38:9

CONSIDER THIS

- "Take delight in the LORD, and he will give you your heart's desires." —Psalm 37:4
- "I have learned the secret of living in every situation. . . . For I can do everything through Christ, who gives me strength." —Philippians 4:12-13
- "This same God who takes care of me will supply all your needs from his glorious riches, which have been given to us in Christ Jesus." —Philippians 4:19

CONSIDER THIS

- Do I place too many expectations for my happiness on someone else?
- Have I asked God to fulfill my longings and satisfy my needs?
- What are some ways I can begin to trust God more fully to handle my expectations and needs?
- Do I believe God will really complete me? If not, why not? If so, what has been holding me back from fully embracing this truth?
- Do I practice living with a humble and giving mind-set— being self-aware of the impact and responsibility I have toward others?

changing course

When one door closes another door opens, but we so often look so long and so regretfully upon the closed door, that we do not see the ones which open for us.
—ALEXANDER GRAHAM BELL

FOR SEVERAL YEARS I lived in a predominantly Amish area, not far from Tuscarawas County, Ohio, where *Old Fashioned* was filmed. Driving country roads, I had to be on the lookout for any horse and buggy that might be just over the hill. And it was always amusing to see a horse rail in front of the Sugarcreek McDonald's.

So in recent years as Amish fiction has exploded on the literary scene, I've understood some of the intrigue: a simpler life, a strong community feel, and a clear understanding of traditions and boundaries. It's like stepping back into the 1800s.

The reality is that most of us are not going to give up our current lifestyle to live like we're back in another century (I appreciate air-conditioning and microwaves too much for that!), but going back to the traditional ways of treating one another *is* worth considering.

The old fashioned way is about getting back to basics and making virtue heroic. It's about focusing on the heart and character of the other person first and foremost. It's about honoring who that person is as someone who is created in the image of God. It's about the Golden Rule: do to others as you would have them do to you (see Matthew 7:12). That ultimately focuses on living with intention and self-awareness, not tugging on the hearts of those we don't really see a future with.

A friend of mine told me of an experience he had with this "I" and "Thou" relationship. Not long ago he was visiting a tourist area and saw something that made him think of an old girlfriend. He took a photo of it to send to her. It was an innocent moment when he was thinking of her in a pleasant way, and he knew she would appreciate the photo. "But I knew if I sent it to her," he said, "that would be an emotional tug on her heart. What would the gesture of sending that picture mean to her? I had to think about not only my intentions, but also her perception. I chose not to send it. It took me far too many years even to begin to genuinely learn that lesson."

You may think, *What's the big deal?* On a certain level, this action hurts no one. But is that really true? We have to pause and consider how it might affect the other person and what message we're sending. How would it tug at that person's heart?

I'm asking you to push aside the surface stuff in your relationship and focus on the eternal stuff, the stuff that really matters—the stuff that makes a relationship stick together and grow through even the toughest circumstances. That's ultimately what makes for a successful marriage.

When I first got married, I thought life was going to be sex, sex, sex and we were going to do fun things all the time and everything was going to be easier because I had someone to do life with. (I think everyone goes into marriage knowing that not to be true, but still somehow thinking their marriage will be different.) The physical and the fun sides are great, but they're such a small part of real-life marriage. The bigger part is the mundane and routine. Paying the bills and figuring out finances. Housework loads. Work and church and family responsibilities. Those aspects of life and marriage do not require gym-perfected bodies or the latest, hippest . . . anything. They require respect and honorability. They require character.

Wow, those things—like chastity—aren't sexy! But I don't necessarily want sexy when I'm dealing with a child who is sick or a dog who has just ripped apart $300 speakers. I don't want sexy when the doctor has found a suspicious lump. I want someone there I can count on. Someone I can trust. And I want to be that person for someone else.

Cue the sound track. I know that sounds nice. And I know that's the type of person you're ultimately looking for too. But here's the secret: that type of person doesn't simply show up at the altar. If the character stuff isn't a real focus before your wedding day, then it may not be there later. I'm not suggesting a person won't come through for you, but if you don't really know before you get married—and haven't seen it tested—then after you get married, you won't know for certain until the proverbial rubber hits the road. And is that really the time when you want to discover the truth?

The old fashioned way is as much about "becoming" a person of character as it is about "looking" for a person of character. We have to ask ourselves, *How do I develop my own character? How do I really do that, practically?* And doing so will help us better recognize good character in another person.

So what does all this mean for you today?

It means you need to be willing to leave the baggage of your past relationships behind. Learn from them, then let them go. Be willing to take a chance and start over.

If you're in a relationship now and it has gone off the tracks, I'm not suggesting you break up and find someone new. I know people who start messing up in their relationship—they get prematurely physical, for instance—and feel that since they've ruined their perfect love story, they have to quit and walk away. Sometimes you do have to sever a relationship. Sometimes, though, it may not be that the relationship has to be over; it just has to come under scriptural authority or become accountable in some way.

Along with letting the baggage go, we need to evaluate our current assumptions—both from culture and from within the church. Is abstinence unhealthy? What about materialism? The death of monogamy? Do we really believe we have those assumptions right?

From there, we have to determine that others won't hold us back. No matter what they say or think or do, we will choose to live our lives by a different standard. We won't toy with others' emotions or lead them into thinking a relationship is possible if we know it isn't, for instance.

I know that sounds easier than it actually is. We have to fight for what is good and pure. I mean, really, how do you make abstinence or restraint of passion sexy? Or chastity—how do you make that sound sultry and seductive? How do you compete with the overwhelming avalanche of media that encourage unbridled erotic pursuits and pass those off as love?

Swimming against the stream is exhausting sometimes. Although purity is still at least somewhat valued among women (though not as much as in the past), too often if a man tries to live purely and keep his passions in check, he may actually have his sexuality questioned.

The old fashioned way is in some respects a counterintuitive way. There is a kind of love that is indeed almost otherworldly and that can be pursued and achieved no matter your starting place (whether you have never dated or you've been divorced multiple times). That's the beautiful part of the process: it may have boundaries, but within those boundaries permeates a powerful grace to help us overcome our mistakes and to strengthen us to continue in our desire not to settle for something less. And then change is truly possible.

The LORD is for me, so I will have no fear. . . . Yes, the LORD
is for me; he will help me.

—PSALM 118:6-7

CONSIDER THIS

Are You Ready to Change Course?

I am ready to . . .

1. Commit to doing relationships differently.
2. Leave the baggage of my past relationships behind.
3. Challenge the current cultural assumptions about relationships.
4. Refuse to let others hold me back.
5. Believe change is possible.

If you agreed to the above statements, then you're ready to start
living the old fashioned way.

what do you want?

No one gets good at anything without practice. Everything I do now is preparing me for the kind of husband I'll be one day, God willing.

—CLAY, *OLD FASHIONED*

I LOVE THINKING ABOUT THE FUTURE and what it holds—so much promise and potential. I also know that I want to be prepared for the future when it arrives! For me, that's about creating a vision and a mission. In other words, setting goals. Every morning, I pull out a clean sheet of paper and write that day's goals and to-dos. There's something empowering about marking items off the list. I feel that I've accomplished something worthwhile when I do that. Of course, I always have goals that get carried over to the next day. But that's okay. I know I'm working toward something.

There's another set of goals that I'd carried around from the time I was in junior high school: *husband, kids, nice house . . .*

There's nothing wrong with that list of goals. Actually, all my female friends had those same goals! I know men have some similar goals: perhaps *a family, a good career, friends, a solid reputation.* Those are good goals—family, shelter, relationship, work.

But as I grew older and progressed into my thirties, I wasn't ful-filling those goals. And I found that sometimes I would become so preoccupied with that goal list (especially the husband part) that I would get distracted from the more important goals, those that deal with character—patience, gentleness, kindness, self-control.

While some goals are easily checked off (laundry, bills, walking the dog), character goals are never completely checked off. I have yet to honestly say, "Patience, check; gentleness, got it; humility, yep, definite check."

Okay, well, maybe the humility part . . .

When I focused on the husband goal, I found I became a little more short tempered and impatient toward my boyfriend and toward others. When I would receive yet another bridal shower invitation, I wasn't exactly jumping up and down with joy over my friend's happi-ness. Not really attractive traits for snagging the man of my dreams. But when I focused on the goals that would build my character, I found that I was a more joyful person. My relationships got better (all of them, not just with members of the opposite sex).

Ultimately the goal isn't to snag a spouse or learn tricks that will help us manipulate others into giving us what we want. The goal is to love others more fully and, as a result, to become the kind of person who will be ready to recognize and appreciate genuine romantic love when it presents itself.

Mahatma Gandhi is often credited with saying, "Be the change that you wish to see in the world." That's a tall order—and realisti-cally, it's one we can't do without supernatural help. Fortunately Jesus reminds us, "With God everything is possible" (Matthew 19:26).

It's time to set some goals. What are the true goals you want? A spouse? That's an okay goal. How will you meet that goal? By losing ten pounds, wearing great clothes, getting your teeth bleached, and hanging out at the local swing dance club? Or is it perhaps by focus-ing on the more eternal qualities, such as the fruit of the Spirit (love, joy, peace, patience, kindness, goodness, faithfulness, gentleness, and self-control)?[1]

I know, that was a setup. But think about it: you can get yourself in the best shape and do all the "right" things and still not get married. You'll be thin and have a closet full of wonderful clothes, but you still won't have reached your goal. Or you can strive for becoming more loving and compassionate—basically training to become the best spouse you can be. Although it won't guarantee you a life mate, it will certainly guarantee a lifetime of being a person you can be proud of.

> Let us strip off every weight that slows us down, especially the sin that so easily trips us up. And let us run with endurance the race God has set before us. We do this by keeping our eyes on Jesus, the champion who initiates and perfects our faith.
>
> —HEBREWS 12:1-2

JOURNAL

Journal your answers to these questions:

- Who do I want to be?
- What do I really want? What am I really looking for?
- How do my wants affect who I want to be?
- What goals should I set to reach those things?
- If my goal is to be married, how am I preparing myself?

CONSIDER THIS

Psalm 1:1-3 says,

> Oh, the joys of those who do not
> follow the advice of the wicked,

> or stand around with sinners,
> or join in with mockers.
> But they delight in the law of the LORD,
> meditating on it day and night.
> They are like trees planted along the riverbank,
> bearing fruit each season.

What does this psalm tell us about the kinds of goals we should set for ourselves? Will pursuing those goals lead us closer to the right person to share our lives with?

begin again

The way you carry ancient, crusty, useless guilt—like a spoiled pet poodle you want to show off. Like an excuse. Let it go. What are you waiting for? How long?

—AUNT ZELLA TO CLAY, *OLD FASHIONED*

IN THE MOVIE *OLD FASHIONED*, Clay struggles with some of the things he's done in the past. He wants to be a better person. He wants to be "righteous," as some would say. But the bar is so high and the memories of the past weigh so heavily that he has a difficult time moving beyond them.

I can identify with Clay. I know my weaknesses and failings all too well. And I detest them. I see where I want to be, where I should be. I measure how far the distance is from where I am, and I can feel frustrated and helpless.

Yesterday's reading was about the importance of setting the right goals and preparing ourselves for who we really want to be. But maybe you're like me: every time I fall short, I carry the burden of that failure and it spirals into insecurity, which, if I don't get ahold of it, can take a nosedive into hopelessness.

My head knows God loves me, that he desires the best things for me, that life is a journey, a process, in which I'm *always* striving to grow and stretch and become more like who God would have me to be. My heart, however, sometimes receives a flawed, skewed message instead: *I'll never be the kind of person someone wants to be with. What is wrong with me? Why can't I do this? I'm unlovable. I'm unworthy. . . .*

These are lies. They're dangerous thoughts that can damage our emotional and spiritual health, our relationships, and even our faith. Beyond embracing the truth, we need to take these thoughts captive (see 2 Corinthians 10:5) and combat them head-on.

If you are currently involved in unhealthy behaviors or patterns that could be jeopardizing what you really want, then it's time to stop and commit or recommit to living a different way—a healthy way.

It's easy to think about our weaknesses in terms of crossing physical boundaries. But what about other areas? Times when we're too needy or insecure? Too demanding? Possessive? Times when our attitudes or words get us into trouble?

The apostle Paul understood these things clearly when he said, "Forgetting the past and looking forward to what lies ahead, I press on . . ." (Philippians 3:13-14).

Forgetting the past.

Looking ahead.

Pressing on.

Beginning again. As many times as it takes.

Here's the thing to remember—especially when we begin again and again and again: God created us. He knows our weaknesses and how fragile we are. He knows we will mess up. What does he want from us? He wants us to run back to him every time. We don't have to wait to fix ourselves before we approach him to start anew. The Bible reminds us that God loved us and Christ died for us "while we were still sinners" (Romans 5:8)—while we were messing up and rebelling and doing things our own way. So our weaknesses don't surprise him. At. All.

What an amazing thing: our past doesn't have to determine our future. We don't have to stay stuck. We can be different. Even in the midst of our failures, we can begin again. That's what I love about traditions and routines—they always begin again. Just as the sun comes up in the east every morning and sets in the west every evening. Just as December 25 comes every year. Or we sing "Take Me Out to the Ball Game" during the seventh-inning stretch at baseball games. We gain the opportunity to start afresh—every single day.

Although we can't control how other people view or treat or even think about us, we can stand tall and confident in Jesus. We can be steadfast in the truth of who we are in light of what God has done for us through Christ and seek the help and wisdom of God and others in our quest to begin again.

And since we know there are no quick fixes (those goals keep us focused and bring us back on track), we can and must be merciful to ourselves and to others. We need to remember we're all on a journey. Beginning again doesn't mean escaping the consequences of our actions or avoiding responsibility when it's in our power to act. But God offers mercy and strength along the way.

This is especially important in our romantic relationships as we build toward marriage. Because marriage is more intimate emotionally, spiritually, and physically, it offers us more opportunities for growth *and* for failure, for celebration *and* for forgiveness.

Decide right now, the next time you flub up (and trust me, there will be a next time), you won't give up on yourself and call it quits. You won't surrender. You won't wallow in it. You won't carry the guilt. But instead, in humility and determination, you will let it go. You'll ask God (and others, if you need to) for forgiveness and press on, "looking forward to what lies ahead."

The word of the LORD holds true, and we can trust everything he does.

—PSALM 33:4

CONSIDER THIS

No Buts *Allowed!*

Read these Scripture verses at face value and contemplate what they say to you. And don't allow your mind to add a "Yes, but . . ." at the end.

- "[God] has removed our sins as far from us as the east is from the west." —Psalm 103:12
- "You are precious to me. You are honored, and I love you." —Isaiah 43:4
- "The faithful love of the LORD never ends! His mercies never cease. Great is his faithfulness; his mercies begin afresh each morning." —Lamentations 3:22-23
- "By [Christ's] one offering he forever made perfect those who are being made holy." —Hebrews 10:14

JOURNAL

Write about some of the things you'd like to forget. Ask God to help you move beyond those things. What mental shift can you make today to change the course of your thought patterns, relationships, and self-worth so you can move forward into a better, stronger future?

respect yourself

R-e-s-p-e-c-t, find out what it means to me. . . . Oh, sock it to me, sock it to me, sock it to me . . .

—ARETHA FRANKLIN

AND NOW SOMETHING for those on the other side of pride . . . a word to the broken or lost.

One of my favorite parts of the movie *Old Fashioned* is Amber's character progression. At the beginning we see glimpses of her past baggage and how that has affected the way she views herself. But as the movie progresses, we see Amber grow more into a woman who respects herself and accepts that she can and should value who she is.

In one scene with her coworker Carol, she explains her MO.

"When life gets messy, I move on," Amber says. "That's what I do. I'm good at it."

"What happens when you run out of places to move on to?" Carol asks.

"The world is pretty big."

"It's pretty messy, too. Everywhere," Carol tells her.

In another scene, Clay questions Amber's money jar.

Amber explains, "When the jar is full, I know I have enough."

"For what?" Clay asks.

"To get far enough away, if I need to. Make a fresh start. Go where the wind takes me. Follow the warm fuzzies."

Sounds nice. When life gets too complicated or frustrating or painful, I've often daydreamed about chucking everything and moving somewhere else to start over. The problem is that *I* go with me. The things within me that are broken—my past baggage, my weaknesses, my character flaws—all come right along with me and settle in at the new place.

There's enough here to keep a psychologist in business for decades, so I'll focus on only one aspect of this that gets to the old fashioned things we've lost: respect for ourselves and who we are in Christ.

I know I've often worked so hard to respect other people that I've allowed them not to respect me. When we don't have a healthy understanding of who we are in Christ—valuable, worthy, loved children of God—then we may struggle with respecting ourselves and confidently requiring that others respect us. We deserve to be treated with respect and honor—because we are made in God's image, because before we were even born, he knew us (see Jeremiah 1:5). He has our name tattooed on the palm of his hand (see Isaiah 49:16).

God loves you. Do you believe that?

No, really. Do you?

Before you were born, he saw into the future. He saw your absolute rock-bottom, worst moment.

And he *still* gave his life for you.

You are loved.

When we truly begin to grasp that, we grow in confidence, but also we begin to appreciate, accept, and respect who we are. Right now. And who we can be. And we understand that both of those (our current and our future selves) are connected. Both are loved. Both deserve respect—from ourselves.

It's amazing how that understanding begins to shape our outlook, our decisions, our mentality and attitude. It becomes easier to place healthy boundaries and stand firm and unapologetic in those.

We don't have to compromise what we believe. The temptation to lower our standards often sneaks up on us. It may come when we begin to doubt God's plan for us. We watch other people walking down the matrimonial aisle and wonder, *Will I ever find the right person to marry?*

This can become especially tricky when we opt to lower our standards (to disrespect ourselves) and date someone who doesn't share our same core values and beliefs. It makes sense if dropping that requirement widens the dating pool, right?

But it ends up hurting us more than making us stronger. In a 2000 study published in the *Journal of Family Issues*, researchers found that "deeply religious men" far less commonly live with a woman before marriage than nonreligious men. But "deeply religious women" are just as likely to live with a man as nonreligious women. Why?

One of the researchers suggested, "My theory is that women are willing to make sacrifices for their partners, once they have become emotionally attached. They're willing to make compromises to try to hang on to the relationship. Men won't do that. . . . These girls are probably thinking, *He's not perfect. But I love him and I can help him change.*"[1]

While we may offer the excuse "But this is *different!*" the reality is that we may utter that excuse because we've forgotten the importance, power, and patience that come from respecting ourselves.

Self-respect doesn't have to be just holding firm to the physical boundaries. I know women who are virgins but who allow men to string them along emotionally. And I know of men and women who, in their own insecurity, string others along emotionally. They tug at the hearts of others in small ways that can become manipulative and that may be unintentional.

We see this same struggle over respect in the movie *While You Were Sleeping*. Sandra Bullock's character, Lucy, starts to fall in love with the brother of a man she was initially attracted to but who is now in a coma. When she and the brother have a misunderstanding and Peter, the coma guy, wakes up and asks her to marry him, she decides to accept. She slaps down a sticky-note wedding invitation on her boss's desk, which he reads and then says confusedly, "You're marrying the coma guy? What happened to the other guy?"

She tearfully replies, "He didn't want me."

Lucy was willing to give up on herself and her dreams and everything she longed and worked for to have a cheap imitation.

It is okay to have standards and hold to them confidently and assuredly. It is okay to protect your personal boundaries and to say no and have it actually mean no.

You are worthy of dignity and respect. It doesn't matter what your baggage from the past is or what your weaknesses are or mistakes have been. God created you for a purpose, and he has plans for you that involve respecting and honoring the gifts, personality, and dreams he has invested in *you*.

> Come to me with your ears wide open. Listen, and you will find life. I will make an everlasting covenant with you. I will give you all the unfailing love I promised to David.
>
> —ISAIAH 55:3

PRAYER

God, sometimes I struggle with who I am and feeling confident in that. My mind drums up all the bad things that have happened to me or that I have done to others, and it feels like I stay stuck in regret and longing and impatience rather than moving ahead into a clear, clean future. Sometimes I disrespect myself by making compromises. Help me to discern when I'm doing that, and help me to be strong and stand firm in valuing and respecting who you made me to be.

JOURNAL

Write about some of the compromises you've made in the past and why you made them. Using your 20/20 hindsight and wisdom, write how you would have counseled and mentored the younger you to do things differently to respect yourself better. Now read what you just wrote and write about how you can apply that same insight to your life today.

CONSIDER THIS

Is it possible to have too much self-respect or self-esteem? What about spiritual pride? Pride can sneak up on us, so that even our insecurity, when we give in to it, becomes a source of pride. Having a healthy self-esteem brings a healthy confidence. It doesn't, however, bring self-centeredness. Self-absorption isn't the same as true, biblical self-respect.

serving the "thou," not the "i"

There is one thing and I'm talking only one thing that, without fail,
no red-blooded woman alive on this planet or any other can resist.
Are you listening? Indifference.

—LUCKY CHUCKY, *OLD FASHIONED*

SALLY (NOT HER REAL NAME) WAS A LOVELY, funny, intelligent woman who never seemed to be at a loss for a date. The problem was that she also couldn't stay in a relationship very long. I could never understand that—until I saw her with her boyfriend. Then it became clear. She never let him finish a sentence, or she would constantly correct him. She would make comments about his opinions and criticize his decisions. I couldn't help feeling sorry for the guy, and I wasn't surprised when not too long after our meeting, they broke up.

Respect for the other. It's just as important as respect for self.

It's something we can easily identify in other people's relationships, and it's something we can target when it's absent. But it's easy to overlook a lack of respect in our own dealings with people. And there are few things we can do in a relationship that are more damaging than belittling or criticizing someone in front of others.

We long for people to use the Golden Rule when dealing with us, but we might not always be so steadfast in applying it to them. This is particularly true if we don't have a deep respect for ourselves, as we discussed in yesterday's reading. When we understand that we are unique and valuable creations of God—when we truly grasp that *for ourselves*—then we can more easily apply that understanding to others, knowing that *they also* are unique and valuable creations of God.

God loves them. He has a plan for them. He desires good things for them. As deep and wide as his love is for us, so also does he love them.

When we grasp that knowledge, doesn't it make our interactions with them different? We don't have to agree with them. We don't even have to like them! But remembering that God loves them so much he gave his Son as a sacrifice for them, too, allows us the freedom to be able to offer them dignity and respect. We can hold others in high opinion and with reverence. We can treat them kindly.

It isn't always easy, but the apostle Paul reminds us, "If it is possible, as far as it depends on you, live at peace with everyone" (Romans 12:18, NIV). As far as it depends on *you*. Not the other people. We aren't accountable for how others live, but we *are* accountable for our own decisions and actions. Even our own words! Jesus was so serious about how we treat others that he told us, "Every careless word that people speak, they shall give an accounting for it in the day of judgment" (Matthew 12:36, NASB).

We treat others with dignity just because they are loved and treasured by God. They don't have to like Chinese food or sci-fi movies. They don't have to like reading or knitting or hunting. They don't have to dress the way we prefer. They don't have to be *anything* like us. Ultimately, those things don't matter. What matters is the way we treat them.

So how do we offer respect?

One way is to listen more than we speak. Without criticizing or judging others, we can ask them honest questions about themselves and then actively listen to find out what makes them tick and why they believe the way they do. Even after understanding, we may still not agree or like them, but we can treat them with reverence. And the more willing we are to accept differing perspectives (that doesn't mean we're soft on morality!), the more we can grow and learn to appreciate those differing perspectives.

For instance, one of my best friends is of a different political party. I don't agree with her perspectives on everything politically. But I enjoy listening to her views so that I can learn why she believes the way she does. The cool part is that as I listen and learn from her, she feels valued and heard, and I solidify the reasons why I vote for the other party! We respect each other.

Even if my friend didn't respect my perspective, I can let that go, because I know that I'm responsible only for my own responses.

Let me be clear that I'm not talking about tolerance. Tolerance is simply going along with someone else without rocking the boat or churning up conflict. Tolerance is the catchword that basically says, "I don't care if you morally or spiritually agree with what I'm doing or what I believe; let me be." Respect is saying with integrity and self-control, "I don't agree with your opinion or your action, but I will treat you with dignity and honor because you are made in the image of God."

Especially in a dating relationship, respect is showing appreciation for who the other person is and what he or she does. It's speaking in respectful tones and not coming across harshly or judgmentally.

Being respectful is being trustworthy—keeping our word and our promises. Understanding that others' time is just as important as ours, we make them a priority when we're with them, as though we have nothing else to do or nowhere else to be that's more important than they are.

This is where I know I'm going to get into big trouble, but I'm diving in anyway. I have a couple of friends who are lovely people. I can't stand going out with them, though, because they are constantly on their phones, texting, googling something, checking sports scores, and who knows what else. When I'm with them, I feel as though they're never quite with me. The message they send me is, *You may not be interesting enough company for me, so I'm keeping my phone nearby just in case I need to do something better.*

The next time you're in a restaurant, check out how many people aren't communicating with one another at the table but instead are focusing on their phones. (This may require you to put down *your* phone!) I hate to sound brutal here, but that's incredibly disrespectful to the people we're with. We're telling them they aren't important enough for us to make them a priority. Ouch.

My family and I have started to hold one another accountable for the texting/phoning stuff. My brother-in-law started it by saying, "Well, that's just *ignurnt*." We all laughed—and now we all do it. "Ignurnt! Ignurnt!" We try to keep it light and respectful, while still making the point. And every time, the guilty person smiles and joins the joke—and puts away the phone.

The old fashioned way advocates holding others in high esteem, and respect starts with how we treat people before we even start with romance. Who you are and how you treat others will inevitably seep into your romantic relationship. Treat people as though they matter— because they do. Build them up instead of cutting them down. Put the other person's best interest in mind and then act according to that attitude. God will honor you for it.

Let everything you say be good and helpful, so that your words will be an encouragement to those who hear them.
—EPHESIANS 4:29

QUIZ

How Respectful Are You?

On a scale of 1 to 5, mark how respectful you are in your relationships.

1 = No way
5 = Yes way

1. When I'm with someone and they're telling a story, I interrupt before they're finished so I can add my own similar story.
2. I love my phone. It keeps me connected with the world. Even when I'm out with family or friends, I still like to check to see what else is going on.
3. If someone has a different opinion from mine, I will make a comment about it or try to get them to see they're wrong.

How did you score?

3–6 points: Way to go! You're so respectful, you could teach a class.

7–10 points: You're getting there. You may not always act respectfully, so now is the time to be more aware and put old fashioned values into practice.

11–15 points: Well . . . how do I say this respectfully? You've got some work to do, my friend.

JOURNAL

In the quiz, I mentioned three ways to show (or not show!) respect. Journal about other ways you offer respect and the areas where you fall short. Think about how you see respect or lack of it in other people, and mark those down so you can learn from them.

a word about guilt

We can only be used by God after we allow Him to show us the deep, hidden areas of our own character.

—OSWALD CHAMBERS

IN THE MOVIE *OLD FASHIONED*, CLAY IS BATTLING the ghosts of his past. The things he did to himself and others continue to haunt him and affect his relationships. In many ways he responds by shutting people out and making it more difficult for anyone to grow closer to him. Although he has been forgiven, the guilt weighs so heavily that he's unable to truly forgive himself.

In one scene, his aunt Zella finally confronts him on his guilt and the unattainable standard he has set: "Get over yourself, you and your pain. Stop trying to use the grace of God as a brick wall." And of course, brick walls keep others out, including God. Sometimes the very thing that is good initially (even the pursuit of God and righteousness) can turn into something unhealthy.

We *all* have things in our pasts that we regret. The apostle Paul reminds us, "Everyone has sinned; we all fall short of God's glorious standard" (Romans 3:23). Your "flavor" of sin may be different from mine, but none of us have done everything in our relationships perfectly. We've all messed up.

We are inherently broken and in need of redemption. This isn't a popular or contemporary idea. We prefer to talk about healthy self-esteem without the healthy balance of understanding our brokenness.

Consider how many minefields you've had to navigate in your dating life from puberty until now—not just physically, but emotionally and psychologically. I don't know anyone who has done things perfectly. Some people may appear to have, but I can guarantee you even they have regrets.

The truth is, it doesn't matter what you've done in the past, how you've handled relationships, if you've damaged others or yourself. Maybe you're young enough not to have many regrets over relationships. That's a good thing. Keep walking firm, with the knowledge that at some point, you will likely step off the path—it may not be physically; it may be by dishonoring someone or gossiping or misleading someone emotionally. God's grace is greater than those mistakes and can cover them completely and wipe them out to give you a new beginning, a fresh start.

Unfortunately, many people hold on to past relational mistakes for years, even decades. Why? Why do we seek forgiveness from God, but still cling to the pain and memories? We pray, "God, remember that mistake I made? Remember when I did this thing?" God says, "No. I'm not sure what you're talking about." *God doesn't remember* the sins we've confessed and been forgiven of. David wrote, "He has removed our sins as far from us as the east is from the west" (Psalm 103:12). This is David we're talking about, the king who slept with another man's wife, then shipped the man to the front lines of battle, where David made sure he would be killed.

I'm taking a risk here, but I think your past is probably not *that*. Yet David is considered a man after God's own heart (see Acts 13:22).

Holding on to our regrets is in essence a pride issue. If we've asked God for forgiveness and he has forgiven us, then we are free. If we continue to hold on to that regret or that sin, we are essentially telling God we know ourselves better than he knows us.

Don't let regrets hold you back from what God has for you. Don't allow the past to dictate your future. Acknowledge it and then let it go.

"Come now, let's settle this," says the LORD. "Though your sins are like scarlet, I will make them as white as snow. Though they are red like crimson, I will make them as white as wool."

—ISAIAH 1:18

CONSIDER THIS

- Rik Swartzwelder, the director and screenwriter for *Old Fashioned*, says, "The true test of spiritual maturity is the capacity to truly forgive, not in a flippant way of saying, 'I forgive; it's no big deal,' but in full acknowledgment of what a big deal something is and then forgiving fully anyway." Do you agree? Why do you think he marks forgiveness in that way?
- Living free from guilt sometimes means a daily acknowledgment that we don't have to live with regret. We can learn from it and then let it go. What are some things you feel remorse for? What do you need to let go of?
- Forgiveness doesn't necessarily mean reconciliation. If you're in an abusive relationship, for instance, you can forgive but not necessarily continue in that relationship. Are there any relationships that you need to step away from for your own health and peace of mind?

JOURNAL

Tear a piece of paper from your journal and list each thing you feel regret over: broken relationships, hurtful things you've said or done, etc. Now take that sheet of paper, go somewhere safe, and light the paper on fire. As you watch it burn, remind yourself that you do not have to live any longer under the weight of those regrets.

PRAYER

God, I have done so many things wrong in my life—both to myself and to others. I ache under the weight of those memories and the pain I've caused. I know I've disappointed you. Please forgive me for those things. Help me not to hold myself hostage anymore to the small voices that whisper I can't be forgiven. Make me strong enough to forgive myself and others. Then give me the strength to let it all go and move forward in your grace and plan for me.

why boundaries matter

AMBER: Not even a little kissy-kissy?
CLAY (pointing to his cheek): Just right there 'til the wedding bells.
AMBER: How long have you had this theory?
CLAY: Nine years.
AMBER: Yikes. That's not normal.

—*OLD FASHIONED*

CLAY IS A STICKLER FOR BOUNDARIES. No kissing until the wedding day. No being alone in Amber's apartment with her. Feet at the threshold until she exits the room, then he can enter.

He's pretty strict.

What about you? Have you ever considered where your boundaries are and why they are what they are? Do you hold to strict boundaries or are they fairly loose, depending on the person you're with and the situation?

Often we neglect to think about boundaries until we're in the middle of needing them! Making a choice in advance is essential for succeeding. We make mistakes far before the moment of the actual "fall." We have to commit to how we'll act in any given situation before getting there in order even to have a chance.

I always thought I was a strong person where boundaries are

concerned. But I discovered that strong boundaries mean constant vigilance. For instance, right after college I got an acting job at a professional summer theater and got involved with a fellow actor. He was looser on his morals than I was. While I was able to say no to sex, he was persistent in pushing my limits.

Then one afternoon on our day off, we visited a fair and were walking arm in arm and enjoying each other's company when a man approached us and handed us a brochure discussing the evils of pornography. My boyfriend pushed it back into the man's hand and said, "No thanks. I see nothing wrong with pornography."

I felt sick inside. I didn't say anything, though, because I didn't want to cause an argument. Really, I didn't want to stop dating this guy either; I liked him, even though I knew he wasn't right or good for me.

Fortunately, it was only a "summer romance," and I was able to keep most of my physical boundaries in place. But what if the relationship had continued? Would he have persistently pushed the boundaries? Would I have gone along, feeling guilty, knowing what I was doing was wrong but allowing it anyway?

Looking back, I wish I could have gotten hold of my younger self and given her a good talking to and perhaps a throttle or two. What regrets I could have avoided. What spiritual darkness I could have stayed out of.

I would have quoted Martin Luther King Jr: "Our lives begin to end the day we become silent about things that matter."

I would have quoted Elisabeth Elliot from her book *Passion and Purity*:

> I took it for granted that there must be a few men left in
> the world who had that kind of strength. I assumed that
> those men would also be looking for women of principle.
> I did not want to be among the marked-down goods on the

bargain table, cheap because they'd been pawed over. Crowds collect there. It is only the few who will pay full price. You get what you pay for.[1]

It isn't only physical boundaries that matter; emotional boundaries are just as important to keep in place (we'll discuss those more in depth in tomorrow's reading).

I know a lot of Christians who want to keep boundaries and yet still try to find a way around them. "Technical virginity" is one way, they believe. But as one friend told me, "I never even knew what 'technical virginity' was until after I became a Christian. The idea that *this* was okay, but *that* wasn't. People were playing games with those lines."

It's important to understand that purity and virginity aren't always the same thing. Purity isn't just about maintaining our own boundaries and protecting ourselves. The old fashioned way calls us to be concerned about other people's boundaries as well. In other words, we need to be aware of arousing desire in the other person.

It's natural to want to be desired. I think this is especially difficult for women because we want to be respected, yet we also want men to desire us. And men are trying to control their urges and still honor women. When we set boundaries, we say, "I want to honor this person. Therefore, I need to respect this person's self-control and relationship with God." We know what regrets feel like. Do we want to participate in causing someone else to experience regret and disconnect in their relationship with God?

We get into trouble when we forget that there's a significance and role we play beyond what's happening in the here and now. The apostle Paul reminds us, "We are not fighting against flesh-and-blood enemies, but against evil rulers and authorities of the unseen world, against mighty powers in this dark world, and against evil spirits in the heavenly places" (Ephesians 6:12).

We are at war, and our souls are at stake. Ignoring the boundaries that God set in place for our protection, health, and joy ultimately puts our souls on the front lines of danger. Being old fashioned isn't meant to include beating ourselves over the head with legalism. It isn't negative or pessimistic. It's being a realist about the world—and not just other people in the world outside us, but the world within us. Being old fashioned isn't about being willfully naive. It's having eyes wide open to the reality of humanity. Old fashioned boundaries help us understand the deadly seriousness of the stakes and then keep us protected.

I'm not going to tell you what your boundaries are. Obviously, the Bible offers us clear nonnegotiables for our relationships. So often our consciences really do tell us where lines are, and God gave us common sense for a reason. It's up to us to decide whether we'll choose to listen.

Not everyone's boundaries are going to be the same. Someone might, because of life experience, feel called to one way, and another might be called to a different limit. For Clay, the door threshold was his limit. He understood that our bodies are designed for certain things and that one thing naturally progresses to the next. For him, being alone with a woman was the beginning of that progression, and so in order to avoid even the temptation it presented, he chose a stricter boundary. That may not be true for everyone.

Take some time and dive into the Bible to see what God has to say about boundaries in our relationships. Have an open mind and heart as you read, and ask God to give you wisdom and a healthy discernment about where your protective limits need to be.

Don't excite love, don't stir it up, until the time is ripe—
and you're ready.

—SONG OF SOLOMON 8:4, *THE MESSAGE*

JOURNAL

Write about what specific things you hold boundaries for. Are there any boundaries you have eased up on or disregarded? Why? How did you feel afterward? Write about those feelings as reminders of the importance of boundaries.

CONSIDER THIS

- What is the goal of creating boundaries? Is the goal to love and protect the other person? Why are boundaries important to your relationships with others, yourself, and God?
- Do you believe, as the apostle Paul says, that we are in a spiritual battle for our souls and that includes the battle of boundaries in relationships? Why or why not?
- Is this world a battleground or a playground?
- What do you think happens to us spiritually when we keep boundaries? When we push them?
- Think about Clay's boundaries that I described. Are they too much? Why do you think he felt the need to keep them so strict? How would you respond to a potential dating relationship if the other person had those same kinds of boundaries?

CONSIDER THIS

Practicing Healthy Boundaries

Check out some of what the Bible has to say about our boundaries:

- "Love each other with genuine affection, and take delight in honoring each other." —Romans 12:10
- "We who are strong must be considerate of those who are sensitive about things like this. We must not just please

ourselves. We should help others do what is right and build them up in the Lord." —Romans 15:1-2

- "You say, 'Food was made for the stomach, and the stomach for food.' (This is true, though someday God will do away with both of them.) But you can't say that our bodies were made for sexual immorality. They were made for the Lord, and the Lord cares about our bodies." —1 Corinthians 6:13
- "Don't look out only for your own interests, but take an interest in others, too." —Philippians 2:4
- "Put to death the sinful, earthly things lurking within you. Have nothing to do with sexual immorality, impurity, lust, and evil desires. Don't be greedy, for a greedy person is an idolater, worshiping the things of this world." —Colossians 3:5
- "Since God chose you to be the holy people he loves, you must clothe yourselves with tenderhearted mercy, kindness, humility, gentleness, and patience. Make allowance for each other's faults, and forgive anyone who offends you. Remember, the Lord forgave you, so you must forgive others. Above all, clothe yourselves with love, which binds us all together in perfect harmony." —Colossians 3:12-14
- "Run from anything that stimulates youthful lusts. Instead, pursue righteous living, faithfulness, love, and peace. Enjoy the companionship of those who call on the Lord with pure hearts." —2 Timothy 2:22

emotional promiscuity

AMBER: What do you want out of life?
CLAY: To be decent. That's it. A good person.
AMBER: Are you for real? What's the catch?

—*OLD FASHIONED*

MANDY (NOT HER REAL NAME) had been in a committed relationship for five years when her boyfriend broke up with her. He was interested in someone else and wanted to pursue a relationship with the other person. Mandy was devastated.

"I knew they were friends," she said. "He would mention her every once in a while. But I never thought anything of it. I thought he was committed to me."

While the church has emphasized the importance of singles maintaining physical boundaries, unfortunately that emphasis has overshadowed a sneakier behavior: emotional promiscuity. The lines for emotional entanglement are not as obvious.

We can practice this behavior often without even realizing it or without understanding the power that emotions have on us. Truly, physical boundaries are a small thing in comparison with emotional boundaries and honoring the other person. "Innocent" flirting, candid texting or sexting, chatting online, or engaging in too-personal conversation can lead to emotional bonds that can become harmful.

The line between healthy interaction and toying with emotions can be a fine one—even in friendships. You may have started out as friends, but then feelings developed. Purity is more than just keeping physical boundaries; it's keeping the whole of you pure: emotionally, psychologically, spiritually. That means saving your deepest emotions for your spouse.

Part of emotional entanglement is that we become swept along by our feelings without reining them in. We can lose our perspective and our ability to discern our actions, and then we begin to justify our choices because "I can't help the way I feel."

Brienne Murk, author of *Eyes Wide Open: Avoiding the Heartbreak of Emotional Promiscuity*, suggests that

> emotional promiscuity is when we are careless with our emotions and allow them to control us, rather than the other way around. . . . God created us as three-part beings—body, soul, and heart—and when we're out of balance in any of these areas our whole state of well-being is threatened. We all know the importance of guarding our bodies, being physically fit, eating right, and taking steps to protect ourselves from physical harm. But just how much attention do we give to feeding, exercising, and guarding our hearts and spirits? What many of us don't realize is that our feelings produce emotional (heart), spiritual (spirit), and sexual (body) responses—so we need to thoughtfully rein in those feelings so they lead to wholeness and purity. [1]

Emotional boundaries require responsibility and virtue on our part. Should we never talk or joke with someone of the opposite sex?

I'm not suggesting that. But I know women whose flirting can get them into trouble. As I watch them I see that they flirt because it fills an insecurity they're dealing with. Often we play fast and loose with someone's emotions because it temporarily soothes an ache we have, an insecurity we're dealing with.

Yet those types of emotional connections are imitations for what we really need—God to fill the void we have. Only God can truly complete us. But we go after the cheap substitutions that bring only temporary relief.

Being old fashioned causes us to become more intentional about how we interact with others. Since we can't trust our emotions (they're so fickle), we need to keep alert about how easily they'll deceive us. Our calling is to hold fast to what is *true*, not to what changes as often as Congress wants to raise taxes.

This can be such a muddy area. Even as we understand, appreciate, and create physical boundaries, we can be guilty of not guarding our own emotions or protecting the emotions of those we come in contact with. Even being too open to "listen" to a friend of the opposite sex can send the wrong signal. We should all be more vigilant with this, because we are all more vulnerable to this than we'd care to admit. For married couples this may seem obvious, but singles should pay closer attention to protecting the emotional lives of others (and their own) as well.

That means if you know someone is interested in you and you aren't interested in them, you shouldn't do anything to deliberately perpetuate an emotional attachment. It's the hardest thing! I know it feels good when others like us. But while it feeds our ego, it harms the other person's emotional and spiritual life.

Some would argue that in order not to put our hearts in jeopardy or toy with the emotions of others, we should simply not get close. Period. I think the truth stands somewhere in the middle. Going the old fashioned way doesn't mean you insist on extremes, that you can never do any of these certain things. Instead it leaves space for you to find your way, with God leading you. That requires submitting completely to him and asking him to fill your emotional needs.

> Love each other with genuine affection, and take delight in honoring each other.
>
> —ROMANS 12:10

CONSIDER THIS

- Recently I heard about a twelve-step program for "love" addiction. Not sex. "Love." Do you think the addiction is to true love or to emotional entanglements? Why do you think we can so easily fall into emotional entanglements?
- Toying with emotions doesn't happen only in romance; it can happen with any relationship, even in business dealings. Someone may dangle the "carrot" of promotion or bonus pay in front of a person without any intention of really following through. Is that legitimate? How would you feel if a boss did that to you? Connect that with a romance. What are some "carrots" that you may dangle in front of another person?

QUIZ

How "Friendly" Are You?

Think about each statement and decide whether it is true or false in describing you.

1. I have ended relationships because I fell for someone else.
2. I like to flirt. It makes me feel special to receive attention from my flirtations.
3. I make decisions based on my feelings.
4. I have not set clear boundaries to protect myself from getting emotionally entangled.

5. I keep my physical boundaries. That's important enough, so I don't worry too much about emotional promiscuity.
6. I would never fall into the trap of trusting my emotions too much.
7. I share deeply personal things with my opposite-sex friends.

Quiz Responses:

If any of these statements were true of you . . .

1. This means that you've fallen for emotional deception. Recommit to evaluating your motives rationally, asking God to shed light on the areas that most need tweaking.
2. There's nothing inherently wrong with wanting to feel special. God gave us friendships and community to build each other up. But using others' emotions to fill your own need is self-centered and will cause damage to your heart and theirs.
3. Advertising executives and marketers must love you! Get to know yourself and what makes you feel attached to someone. Don't be in a hurry to get too close to someone else.
4. Now is the time to get to work. Establish emotional boundaries and write them down in your journal. The more thorough you can be, the better you can remain above the emotional fray.
5. Bless your heart; you've already fallen into the emotional trap and can't get up. It's time to recommit to getting honest about the dangers of ignoring the warning signs and refocusing on submitting to God's work in building your character.
6. The saying goes, "Pride goes before destruction, and haughtiness before a fall" (Proverbs 16:18). Become vigilant about keeping watch (and read number 5 above).

7. Commit now to stop and to put clear boundaries in place. Find a specific person to share your personal issues with— either a family member, a close friend of the same sex, or a professional counselor, clergy member, or spiritual mentor.

beyond the dating life

ZACH: If I walk up to some female standing in a group of other females at a club, what's the most effective way to pick up the first female?
LUCKY CHUCKY: Hit on her friends.

—*OLD FASHIONED*

THE CHARACTER LUCKY CHUCKY in the movie *Old Fashioned* is a piece of work, isn't he? It isn't just how he views potential "hookups," it's how he views all women—with a measure of disdain and a heaping helping of disrespect. Use them or disregard them.

I've known men and women who have treated people this way: unless you can do something for them, you aren't worth their time.

Without character bashing, I wonder how many of us—myself included—have done the same thing? Maybe not to the same extent as Lucky Chucky, but maybe simply ignoring or not offering some bit of kindness and chivalry when we could have?

Lately I've been thinking a lot about this idea of declaring dignity on other people. Looking at them with the eyes of Christ and valuing them as deeply loved, deeply worthy, deeply treasured creations of God. (We discussed this in Day 10's reading.) When we do that, we no longer view other people for what they can do for us, how they help or hurt our reputation, or if they're worth considering romantically. Instead our relationships become less about us and our pursuits and more about fulfilling a desire to honor God by honoring his loved ones. It's the old fashioned "I" and "Thou" that we've spoken of throughout this book: our focus is on the other person, considering others as better than ourselves (see Philippians 2:3).

Sometimes we can become so focused on the hunt (whether it's to find a mate or a job or any number of things) that we inadvertently hurt or dismiss the people God may have put in our lives to mentor or help us or for us to mentor or help them.

Pursuing the old fashioned way isn't just about dating relationships; it's about how we treat all people, even those we're not trying to impress romantically. How we treat those from whom we want nothing or have little to gain says much about who we truly are. So being old fashioned begins long before we start dating.

Recently I read a comment online from a man who expressed frustration over the messages women send men. He wrote,

> [You] talk about friendship. Forget it. Women at the singles groups I go to are not looking for friends. They are only looking for a date. If they don't want to date you, they give you nothing more than the time of day. Every time I've ever been LJBFed (Let's Just Be Friends) by a woman, she did not want to be friends. This is her way of telling me she wanted nothing to do with me.

My heart broke when I read that. It broke because this man has experienced pain and rejection from women—Christian women. It also broke because I've been on both sides of that experience. I've had LJBF said to me. And I've said it. And although sometimes I really *did* mean it, I'm not proud that I said it to people when I really *didn't* mean it.

On the other hand, did this commenter *really* just want to be friends? *Can* men and women just be friends? What about the duty not to tug at someone's heart or allow any room for hope at all if you know for sure you are *not* interested?

Why do we say it? Perhaps it's because we're uncomfortable with how we relate to members of the opposite sex and we're afraid they will get the wrong idea and think our kindness means something more. Maybe we're just unaware (if not in massive denial or downright dishonest!) about our actual intentions.

Perhaps it's just an easy out to allow us not to have to deal with someone we're not interested in—romantically or otherwise. So we say, "Let's just be friends" and then ignore the person. Basically, we lie.

Obviously, we don't want to mislead anyone into thinking we're interested when we're simply offering a kindness. But we don't want to avoid offering a kindness out of fear we'll be misunderstood. Treating others with dignity and respect is how God calls us to deal with all our relationships. We don't hit on someone else to get the "real" person's attention. We don't lead someone on to make another person feel jealous. We don't dismiss people because they don't help us pursue our goals. We don't date someone whom we're really not interested in until someone better comes along.

Living the old fashioned way moves to take an interest in the other person and offers dignity, *just because* that person matters and is valued by God. That's the beginning of understanding and living out real love.

Think of ways to motivate one another to acts of love and good works.

—HEBREWS 10:24

PRAYER

God, how many times have I treated people with less than the dignity they deserve? How many times have I overlooked someone else's needs because I was too busy being focused on my own? Forgive me for those times, and give me your eyes to see everyone as worthy of time and attention and kindness. Give me your heart that bursts with love and mercy toward those I may have disregarded in the past. Give me your ears to hear the softest whisper of someone in need. And give me your hands to reach out and help.

May I not be so concerned with whether the other person has romantic potential for me, but rather may I be more aware of declaring and offering dignity to anyone and everyone.

can men and women be just friends?

HARRY: You realize, of course, that we could never be friends.
SALLY: Why not?
HARRY: What I'm saying is—and this is not a come-on in any way, shape,
*   or form—is that men and women can't be friends because the sex part*
*   always gets in the way.*
— *WHEN HARRY MET SALLY*

RIGHT OUT OF COLLEGE I had a good male friend who was also a coworker. We hung out together constantly and had a great time. And then I discovered he wanted more than friendship; he wanted to move our relationship to the next level. I didn't want to do that, but I also really didn't want to lose his companionship. So we talked through it, he started to date someone else, and we continued to be friends. And then I started to have feelings for him. It was like a crazy reality TV show; eventually we went our separate ways and our friendship cooled.

Through the years I have had a lot of male friends. And I still do. I find I connect easier with men—probably because I enjoy discussions that don't tend to focus on shoes, shopping, or children. But throughout my single years I found it was difficult to have a deep friendship with a man without some sexual tension seeping in, on either his side or mine. And then the relationship would become awkward and strained.

Thinking that maybe it was just me who struggled with this issue, I asked some of my friends—both men and women—about their experiences. Every single one of them acknowledged that the potential for moving beyond friendship was always something that they noticed. While no one was willing to say we shouldn't have friends of the opposite sex, all of them agreed it was complicated. This is especially true as we get older and remain single.

It's a tricky thing because the odds are high that one person's emotions will end up getting toyed with. At any given point one person can become interested in the other or vice versa. This is a good reason the Bible encourages us to be careful and to "guard your heart above all else, for it determines the course of your life" (Proverbs 4:23).

Is it wrong just to have dinner as friends? Is it wrong to go for the sake of companionship? Is it wrong just to do something for its own sake?

Some people would say there's absolutely nothing wrong with that. Go have dinner. Go see a movie. You're not hurting anyone. You're not betraying anyone or dishonoring the other person or God. Go ahead and seek out friends of the opposite gender.

The old fashioned way questions not whether "platonic" opposite-sex friendships are possible but whether they are what's best for us. And researchers are now wondering the same. In two separate studies, researchers from the University of Wisconsin–Eau Claire looked at opposite-sex friendships of more than four hundred adults between the ages of eighteen and fifty-two. Their findings? Men tended to be more attracted to their female friends than women felt toward their male friends; men overestimated their female friends' attraction to them, while the women underestimated the men's level of attraction; and men had a stronger desire to date their friends than did women.[1]

"Attraction in friendship is happening, and it's persistent," said lead researcher April Bleske-Rechek, associate professor of psychology. "I'd venture to say, based on all our data, that in the majority of (opposite-sex) friendships there's at least a low level of attraction. And if it's coming more from one friend than the other, it's probably the guy."[2]

This explains so many of the recent movies and television shows on this topic in which friends decide to add "benefits" to their relationship. They are platonic friends until the sex thing gets in the way. So the movie's answer to that problem is to get it out of the way by just having casual sex: no strings, no commitment, no messy emotions getting in the way of their friendship. But unfortunately, each time, the couple discovers it isn't possible to wade into those waters without one of them getting hurt.

Like most things, the best path is probably somewhere between complete avoidance and "friends with benefits." But clearly there is a risk here, which means we need to live careful, thoughtful lives, making sure we don't cross a boundary or hurt the other person (or get hurt ourselves!).

Each person is different. Some men can be friends with women, but a different kind of man can't, and vice versa. Am I encouraging you to keep your distance from any deep friendship with a person of the opposite sex? Not necessarily.

But you have to be aware of your influence on others. You might be insecure; you might not fully be aware of how attractive you are to another. The old fashioned way means paying attention at a greater level to your influence, even if the other person says he or she is content with just "friendship." Learning to read between the lines and making the mature call is about as old fashioned as it gets.

The principle of being old fashioned is about understanding how to avoid extremes; being mature in our dealings with others; and being a realist about the world, who we are, and who other people are. More so than a hard-and-fast rule, the old fashioned way suggests that we continually consider how we treat each other. The goal is to care for others with respect and dignity, keeping our hearts, minds, and bodies pure.

> If you keep yourself pure, you will be a special utensil for honorable use. Your life will be clean, and you will be ready for the Master to use you for every good work.
> —2 TIMOTHY 2:21

CONSIDER THIS

Take an honest assessment of each of your opposite-sex friends and answer the following questions:

1. How do I really feel about my opposite-sex friend?
2. Am I attracted to my friend?
3. How does my friend feel about me? Is my friend attracted to me? If so, what makes me believe that?
4. Do I honor boundaries, or do I push them to move the relationship from being platonic?

CONSIDER THIS

Relating in Healthy Ways

1. Minimize any potential sexual tension. Watch being touchy-feely toward your friend—even if you consider yourself a naturally affectionate person. You want to avoid sending the wrong message.
2. Avoid questionable situations. If you want to hang out with your friend in a place where others might consider it a date, simply ask another friend along or don't go as a "couple." Even the difference between meeting for coffee versus noshing together at a fancy restaurant for supper will help keep boundaries clearer.

3. If you and your friend begin to struggle with boundaries, clearly communicate the boundaries and expectations. Then if you're still struggling, decide if the friendship needs to take a break.

the good old days of courtship

AMBER: Flatter me. Excite me. Sweep me off my feet. Tell me I'm the most attractive woman you've ever seen, even if you don't really mean it. I don't care.

CLAY: Lie to you?

AMBER: Exactly. A normal date.

—*OLD FASHIONED*

MORE THAN A DECADE AGO a book hit the market that caused an uproar because of the stance the author took on relationships. The book's title? *I Kissed Dating Goodbye.* The author, Joshua Harris, became so disillusioned with dating practices and how little they promoted purposeful relationships that he quit.

Interestingly enough, a few years later he wrote a book called *Boy Meets Girl: Say Hello to Courtship.* He tripped upon the old fashioned practice of courting and found a richness and purity to it. He discovered that this form of "dating" actually promotes a solid foundation for enjoying a successful and thriving long-term, committed relationship.

What's the difference between dating and courtship?

In simple terms, dating promotes more of a recreational romance. Maybe you're interested in the person as a potential mate, but likely you're more interested in having fun and hanging out. Dating offers you a movie-and-dinner appointment on a Friday night so you aren't sitting alone in your apartment watching *NCIS* reruns. There's nothing necessarily wrong with that; it simply doesn't provide any sort of solid foundation to learn about the other person and discern if this is a person you want to spend the rest of your life with. Dating is, "Hey, let's hang out and see where this goes."

As Clay mentions in *Old Fashioned*, "I don't believe that dating trains us to be good husbands or wives, you know? Life partners. It trains us to be good dates. That's it. Trains us to be skilled in the superficial." We often know how to create a mood and be "romantic." Our culture relentlessly schools us in becoming great dates, not well-equipped and mature, loving mates. So if that's what dating has to offer, what is courtship, and how is it different?

Courtship is more of an intentional and purposeful romance, in which both people seek to determine whether this is the person they want to be committed to for the rest of their lives. It has much clearer boundaries than dating:

- The couple is never alone, just the two of them. They get to know each other in public or group settings, preferably with close friends or family members.
- The couple has no physical contact—no touching, hand-holding, or kissing—until they are married.
- Courting couples agree and state clearly at the beginning of the relationship that their intentions are to see if the other person is a suitable potential spouse.
- They focus on getting to know each other slowly as platonic friends and spiritual companions without physical intimacy or emotions muddying their perspectives.
- Typically, parents are more involved in giving permission and offering advice.

- Couples are dedicated to commitment, purity, and upstanding morality.

Some people find this style of connection overly controlling and oppressive. On the positive side, though, in dating you can get emotionally attached more quickly, which can cloud objectivity, whereas courting allows you to move slowly and methodically, which helps keep hurt feelings and emotional damage more to a minimum.

A lot of people shy away from the idea of courtship because it sounds too much like it leads into arranged marriages. I'm not saying that's true, but even if it is, is that such a bad thing? I know a man whose family arranged his marriage. He and I used to work at the same company until he left to wed the woman his parents chose for him. One day I asked him why he was going through with it.

"In your culture you choose your mate, but look at how that has turned out," he told me. "The divorce rate—even among Christians— is terrible. I've met this woman. She is from a good family, and she loves Jesus. My family knows her and her family. They have chosen well for me and know what I need and want in a wife. Why not trust those who know me best?"

He was looking at marriage and love differently. To him, marriage isn't just about feeling love. He told me, "Feelings are good, but they should not dictate a relationship. Feelings will come and can grow deeper as I choose to act lovingly."

Well, I couldn't argue with that.

Courtship may seem more controlling and structured. But what if, by following this old fashioned practice, you were able to avoid painful breakups and a potential divorce down the road? Obviously, courting someone doesn't guarantee a happy marriage free from doubts, trouble, and arguments. But it certainly builds a good foundation to move you closer to that end.

The best part of courtship? You practice living a careful, thoughtful life that honors God and other people. What could possibly be better than that?

Regardless of whether you date or court, doing things the old fashioned way is no guarantee. You can love and respect someone fully and keep all the boundaries yet still end up being abandoned, abused, or hurt beyond belief. Doing the right thing doesn't mean God owes you anything. That is a legalistic trap that can (and has) led many to run from God after life doesn't turn out the way they expect or feel they deserve. It's important to remember that the old fashioned way is its own reward.

> May the God of peace make you holy in every way, and may your whole spirit and soul and body be kept blameless until that day when our Lord Jesus Christ comes again.
> —I THESSALONIANS 5:23

JOURNAL

Write down how you view the differences between dating and courting.

- What are the strengths of each? What are the weaknesses?
- If you determined to practice courtship, what boundaries and expectations would you want to be put in place?
- How do you think your life and relationships would be different if you decided, *You know what? I'm going to try this.*
- What do you think would happen to you spiritually? Emotionally? Psychologically?

CONSIDER THIS

Part of the old fashioned way is owning one's affections and being public, in the context of community, about one's intentions toward the other. When we "hide away," keeping our relationship from the watchful eyes of those who know us and love us best, we can open a Pandora's box of problems. In what ways are you tempted to hide? In what ways can you pursue a more intentional approach to relationships?

goodness gracious

AUNT ZELLA: I admire you so much. In all my days, I have never seen anyone work harder at being good.

CLAY: Define good.

AUNT ZELLA: There's no such thing as goodness without mercy. No virtue without forgiveness.

—*OLD FASHIONED*

PHIL CONNORS IS A SELF-CENTERED, disgruntled, frustrated TV weatherman who finds himself unavoidably covering a story about Punxsutawney Phil, a groundhog, and a small town's celebration of Groundhog Day. Because of a severe storm, he and his coworkers are forced to spend the night in the town. But something goes terribly wrong, and he awakens the "following" day, and the next, and the next to discover he is reliving the same day over again.

True to his character, he tries to use this newfound discovery to his advantage, since he sees no long-term consequences. He learns everything he can about his coworker Rita in order to seduce her, which of course backfires every time.

Eventually he realizes he has been given a great opportunity to make his life "right." He can become a good person and enrich and care for the lives of others. He gets to that new day, February 3, only when he alters his entire approach to living.

Obviously, this is the synopsis of the movie *Groundhog Day*. Yet it has its basis in the reality of living the old fashioned way. Ultimately this movie shows us the power that comes by changing the way we view our lives. It shows us the potential of goodness.

In goodness, the character traits of morality, virtue, humility, loyalty, and integrity all wrap themselves up.

One theologian defines goodness as "more than an excellence of character; it is character energized, expressing itself in active good." Our motives become about pleasing God in all we do. And although we have failures, ultimately it is "the direction of such a person's desires, his motivations, that gradually determines his character, not necessarily the degree of perfection he has achieved."[1]

First Corinthians 10:24 tells us, "Don't be concerned for your own good but for the good of others." This applies to our dealings with all people, not just the one we're in a dating relationship with. As we practice building goodness in our lives, we will bring into our dating relationship a stronger sense of who we are and why we do what we do. We will become more concerned with the other person's joy than our own.

Goodness isn't simply something we decide to have, though. We grow it—or more precisely, the Holy Spirit grows it within us as we obey his plans for our lives. Goodness is a fruit of the Spirit. Look at what else grows alongside goodness as we invest our commitment to God's will: "The Holy Spirit produces this kind of fruit in our lives: love, joy, peace, patience, kindness, goodness, faithfulness, gentleness, and self-control. There is no law against these things!" (Galatians 5:22-23).

I love fruit: peaches, apples, strawberries, grapes, blueberries. I love it because it's good for me—packed with antioxidants and all sorts of vitamins that keep my body healthy and strong. But more than that, I like fruit just because it tastes so delicious.

Why fruit? Why doesn't the Holy Spirit produce vegetables in us?

Vitamin packed, yes. But there's nothing too sweet about a brussels sprout.

Someone who exhibits the fruit of the Spirit exudes a sweetness that draws others to him or her. The truth is that a great body and an attractive face will draw attention from the opposite sex. But those things fade, and what will be left?

Several years ago I interviewed a famous supermodel. I spent most of the interview going back and forth between asking questions and trying to suck in my stomach to look thinner. But I'll never forget something she said about her marriage.

"When I was dating my husband, he constantly told me I was beautiful. He gave me compliments all the time about my appearance. But now that we're married, he never tells me I'm beautiful anymore."

"*Never?*" I asked. I had a difficult time believing that absolute, especially since this woman was beautiful, even out of her "prime."

She shook her head. "Never."

"So where does that leave you?"

She smiled and pointed to her heart. "I have things that are better than my outward appearance. I have the fruit of the Spirit."

I looked at her again closely. She was older and had some wrinkles. Her face was lovely but not perfect. And then I realized why she was beautiful. Her eyes shone. Her attitude was gentle and kind. She was exuding goodness—ah, that sweet fruit.

Not everyone understands true goodness. But those who follow the path of the old fashioned way do, and they reap a great harvest because of it.

Anyone who belongs to Christ has become a new person.
The old life is gone; a new life has begun!
—2 CORINTHIANS 5:17

JOURNAL

Make a list of the fruit of the Spirit from Galatians 5:22-23: love, joy, peace, patience, kindness, goodness, faithfulness, gentleness, and self-control. Beside each fruit, write how you would define it. What does it mean and look like to you? How does it work in your life? Then write a prayer asking God to produce an overflowing harvest in you.

PUT IT INTO PRACTICE

Read these Bible verses, then set them to memory (or write them on sticky notes and post them around your home and in your car):

- "You sent your good Spirit to instruct them, and you did not stop giving them manna from heaven or water for their thirst." —Nehemiah 9:20
- "Teach me to do your will, for you are my God. May your gracious Spirit lead me forward on a firm footing." —Psalm 143:10
- "I am about to do something new. See, I have already begun! Do you not see it? I will make a pathway through the wilderness. I will create rivers in the dry wasteland." —Isaiah 43:19
- "Keep on asking, and you will receive what you ask for. Keep on seeking, and you will find. Keep on knocking, and the door will be opened to you. For everyone who asks, receives. Everyone who seeks, finds. And to everyone who knocks, the door will be opened." —Luke 11:9-10

chivalry is not dead!

When did treating women with respect become the joke? You wanna laugh at believing love can be something sacred? Go ahead. Laugh.

—CLAY, *OLD FASHIONED*

THE FIRST TIME I met my now-husband, Scott, was at a group outing. We talked briefly, and then before I left, he picked up my coat and helped me put it on.

That's thoughtful, I thought.

The next time we saw each other at another group outing, he again helped me on with my coat, and then he held the door open for me when we left.

Wow, I thought, impressed. *Chivalry isn't dead.*

As we got to know each other and then started to date, I noticed that chivalry is part of his character. He asked to hold my hand the first time; he didn't assume he could just grab it. He holds doors for me. Opens my car door. Always lets me enter a place first. When I'm chilly, he'll take off his jacket and put it around my shoulders. If he goes into the kitchen to get something to drink, he always offers to bring me something as well.

His chivalry swept me off my feet into the most romantic relationship I've ever experienced. After more than twelve years of marriage, he still treats me the same way.

He even extends that courtesy to others. He opens my mother's car door. He helps his mom on with her coat. At an entrance, he'll open a door for other people.

Is chivalry old fashioned? You bet. Is it sexist? Not a chance.

A friend of mine recently accused chivalry as being nothing more than a holdover from when men treated women as property in order to keep them down. Some people might agree. I'd say they don't understand the true old fashioned ideal of chivalry.

Chivalry is just another word for courtesy, politeness, consideration, respect. Are those outdated ideas? Chivalry is the ideal that you treat another person as honored, appreciated, special. It's not about thinking the other person incapable of doing things for herself or taking advantage of some situation; instead, it's showing a heart that wants to serve another person. It's showing a loving action.

I love the old movies in which the man removes his overcoat and spreads it over a puddle so the woman can walk and not get her dress muddied. It's just thoughtful.

Now before you roll your eyes and think, *She thinks she's living in the 1950s*, let me tell you about myself. I'm a feminist at heart. I'm an independent, professional woman who believes in equality. I don't like to be called "honey" by well-meaning waitresses or by coworkers. I'm not fragile or frail. And I try not to use my feminine wiles to get some big strapping man to do something for me. (Although if he wants to change my flat tire, I'll politely accept—but that's more because I just don't like to get dirty.)

But I also appreciate being treated like a lady. I may be equal, but I also appreciate that God designed me to be different from men.

Can I open my own door? Sure. But I like that my husband respects me and wants to show me that respect by offering certain chivalrous acts. He shows me his character and his heart when he does that. He doesn't have to tell me, "I value you." Opening a door is a simple way to show me that value. And that, to me, makes me feel honored—not as some poor, helpless female who lacks the strength to open a door! It makes me feel honored as a person—I'm valued. And my husband shows me that in those small ways. The message I hear is *I value you as a person. I want to honor you by serving you in this small way and sacrificing my desire to be first.* All that just from opening a door!

I've heard women accuse men who try to be chivalrous of being sexist. That's not to say that some men aren't sexist. I've met my fair share. However, I've also noticed that the ones who have acted in sexist ways never opened any doors for me or acted with even an ounce of chivalry. I would offer the guess that perhaps that's because those people tend to think of themselves first and don't offer respect or value to anyone other than themselves. Sexist people aren't giving people. They don't have a heart for helping others or sacrificing their wants for the better good of another person.

I've talked with women who really long to be treated with this kind of value. But our culture doesn't seem to appreciate chivalry or to train men any longer in those ways.

I've talked with men who long to treat women this way, but they worry that it won't be received in the genuine way it is intended. These men don't have the mentality of *I'll open the car door for you and treat you like a lady, but then I expect you to "put out" for me.*

And just so I'm not keeping it one sided: a woman can be sexist too. Women can objectify men just as much as the other way around. We can manipulate to get what we want. Although the idea of chivalry is connected specifically with what men do for women, the definition of it can certainly apply to women as well. We can serve others and give of ourselves for the benefit of others. We can honor and respect. We can think highly of the opposite sex because God created them uniquely and for a purpose.

Chivalry doesn't have to be dead. It doesn't have to express a need to control or a thought that the other person isn't capable of taking care of him- or herself.

If you're in a relationship that doesn't hold chivalry as a high standard, your relationship isn't doomed! You shouldn't break up with a guy who doesn't offer you his jacket when you're freezing. It might be that he doesn't realize the importance of those kinds of actions, because maybe he's never been taught. And maybe you've never thought about being treated that way.

The ideal of chivalry is compatible with Jesus' teachings. It really is as simple as loving and serving the way Christ calls us to. The next time an opportunity arises to put into action a way to show respect and consideration for another person, give it a try. You'll be amazed by how it makes you feel.

[Jesus said,] "Now that you know these things, God will bless you for doing them."

—JOHN 13:17

CONSIDER THIS

- Think about when you do something simple for another person. How does that make you feel? What is the message you're sending?
- How does it make you feel when another person does something simple for you? What message do you receive from that?

PUT IT INTO PRACTICE

- The next time an opportunity arises for you to act chivalrous or to accept someone else's chivalry, do it with an open heart and mind, expressing gratitude for that opportunity of kindness.

- Do you want to be chivalrous but don't know how it will be received? Take a risk and give it a whirl. The more you do, the easier it becomes and the more your heart grows over those simple acts of respect and service.
- Do you long to be treated in chivalrous ways but aren't? Try asking for it. Even a simple, "You know what would make me feel special and valued? If you opened my car door for me. It's not that I can't do it myself, but when you do it, it shows me your care and consideration for me." Then show your appreciation every time it happens. Gratitude goes a long way to encouraging others to take a risk of service.

nobility isn't just for royals

I think the world has enough greatness. Not enough goodness. That's my theory.

—AMBER, *OLD FASHIONED*

ONE OF THE THINGS EVANGELIST BILLY GRAHAM is known for is never being alone with a woman other than his wife. He has even taken it to the extreme of stepping out of an elevator if the only other passenger is female. Billy is serious about his conviction that he needs to guard his integrity and avoid even the appearance of sin (see 1 Thessalonians 5:22).

While most of us don't take things to that extreme, Billy Graham understands something that, in some ways, seems to be lacking in our culture and even in the church. We've lost the appreciation for virtue and nobility.

Obviously, for many years Billy Graham was in a highly visible role that demanded that kind of strictness. And most of us can argue, "Well, I'm no Billy Graham." But I think many singles (and married folk too) forget that, to someone, they probably are.

It's easy for us average Joes or Janes to think that what we do has comparatively little impact. We might think, *Who am I, after all? I'm not a pastor; I'm no great religious leader.* We can even use that thinking as a cop-out, an excuse. We often don't take God's call on our lives seriously enough, or the impact we might have on someone who is watching (even if we don't know it).

In *Old Fashioned*, when Clay refuses to enter Amber's apartment to be alone with her, does it ultimately matter? It does to him. He understands the weakness of his humanness and that those little compromises become a slippery slope. He stands by his convictions and takes the high—and difficult—road. That's virtue. That's nobility. Today, we would call it having integrity.

In some sense part of being noble is acknowledging that the world is a dangerous place—filled with sin and our human nature—and we are all made of the same stuff; because of that, we are on high alert. So an example would be Clay's not being alone with Amber. She could ask him, "Why won't you be alone with me? Don't you trust me?"

And his noble response would be, "No, I don't. And I don't trust *me*, either."

To be sure, nobility doesn't equal perfection. We are still broken people in need of a Savior. So we can be noble and still weak. Even the best, most noble people can fall. Does that eradicate their story and crush their integrity forever? No. That's what is so amazing about grace.

I knew a good, solid, Christian married man who had a very public affair with a good, solid, Christian married woman. It devastated both families. They will struggle in some way with the consequences of that choice for the rest of their lives. However, once they both realized what they'd done, they sought forgiveness and reconciliation. Today, the man teaches character classes in high schools. Some would say, "Ha! How can he teach anything about character?" But perhaps he can teach so strongly about character because of what he's been through. He understands the nobility of nobility, and he's been on the opposite side and seen the devastation of being without it.

You know where your weaknesses lie. In a relationship that's growing closer, you know where your potential is to give in. I'm not suggesting that you should never be alone with a member of the opposite sex. Maybe you don't have to take it to the extreme that Clay or Billy Graham did. Maybe you do. My weakness was being alone in my apartment with my boyfriend late at night. I can tell you I made some decisions in moments of weakness that I wouldn't label virtuous or noble. My head would shout about holding strong to my moral fiber, to my self-respect, and to my respect for him. But my body would rationalize, *Just this once. It isn't really hurting anybody.*

It *does* hurt somebody. Once or a million times, it chips away at my character. It hurts my relationship with God. It raises my tolerance level for sin so that the next time it becomes easier to rationalize.

Being noble, having virtue and integrity, means drawing a line in the sand and saying, "I'm standing firm because I believe in God's boundaries. I know they're put in place for my good and for the good of my relationships." This isn't easy to do! But that's what makes it noble and courageous.

I can honestly say that every time I've stood firm in my convictions— not just about physical things but also about emotional and spiritual things—I've never once felt an ounce of regret.

Those who value truthfulness, politeness, moral strength, and boundaries are irresistible. You can trust them, knowing that if they stood firm in the difficult moments without compromising, the possibility is much stronger that they'll stand firm in a covenant relationship with you. And vice versa. The strongest people are those who know just how weak they are.

This is nobility: to aspire to be good for yourself and others. Even when you mess up, to get back up and start again. To pursue honesty, compassion, selflessness, and boundaries. To hold your head up high, even while others question your old fashioned motives and actions.

Decide how you will act *before* you're put in a difficult situation. Think about what God would have you do, then pray about it and spend time reading the Bible, God's Word, to find the answers.

[God] grants a treasure of common sense to the honest.
He is a shield to those who walk with integrity.
—PROVERBS 2:7

CONSIDER THIS

How Noble Are You?

Honesty is an important part of virtue.
- Do you tell the truth even when it's difficult?
- Do you keep promises? Or do they become empty words?
- Do you tell others what they want to hear or what they need to hear?
- Are you honest about your feelings toward your significant other, or are you using him or her for whatever you feel you can get (companionship, for instance)?
- Do you compromise your standards because it's easier?

CONSIDER THIS

How Noble Is Your Potential Significant Other?

- Can you trust the person you're dating or considering dating? Does he or she keep promises, even when doing so is difficult?
- Do promises become empty words?

- Does the other person tell you what you want to hear or what you need to hear?
- Is he or she honest about feelings, or is this person using you for whatever he or she can get?
- Does the other person compromise his or her—or your—standards?

PUT IT INTO PRACTICE

Think about the people you know who are virtuous or noble. What do you see in them that qualifies them that way? Ask if you can talk with them; then find out how they have committed to being noble, especially in tough situations. Incorporate the principles you learn from them in your own life.

chastity. really?

I can't even remember how many girls I've been with. . . .

—CLAY, *OLD FASHIONED*

MANY YEARS AGO I had a conversation with a coworker in which he informed me that he would never marry someone he hadn't had sex with first. "I need to know that part of the relationship is good," he told me.

I felt like he was talking about looking under the hood of a Buick before he bought it. As though a physical relationship is a car you need to test-drive.

When I mentioned to him that I was still a virgin, he went from awkward silence to gawking to expressing sympathy for my future husband.

I wasn't too surprised by his response. After all, in our culture, the norm is to have sex. According to a 2011 study published by the National Center for Health Statistics, about 97 percent of men and 98 percent of women ages twenty-five to forty-four aren't virgins.[1]

Everywhere we turn, it seems, someone is talking about sex—movies, music, television, car ads. So abstaining from sex places a person way outside the mainstream.

When everybody is "doing it," we can feel like the butt of someone's joke: "Wait, you're a virgin? Seriously? What's wrong with you?"

And like my coworker, it seems that most people believe it's essential to know what you like in sex before you can possibly vow to spend the rest of your life with one person—who will be the last person you have sex with.

Even in the movie *Old Fashioned*, Amber questions Clay's decision not to partake in that particular activity:

"No one gets good at anything without practice," Clay says. "Everything I do now is preparing me for the kind of husband I'll be one day, God willing."

"What about sex?" Amber asks.

"What about it?"

"That takes practice too," Amber says.

Amber reveals our cultural attitude that is based on the idea that sex is primarily about what satisfies us, which suggests that sex's primary purpose is pleasure. I've even heard of some spiritual leaders who don't think there's anything wrong with it outside of marriage— as long as the couple is committed to each other and loves each other. It's as though they're shrugging in defeat and admitting, "Well, they're going to do it anyway, so why fight it?"

I'll be the first to admit that if you look at sex purely from a pleasure point of view, it makes sense not to wait. Why in the world *would* you?

And the church typically just says to save sex for marriage, without acknowledging the discrepancy between puberty (when nature says we're ready for sex) and the increasing average age for marriage (which is now in the upper twenties). A friend recently told me, "I didn't grow up in the church. And my formative years were far from virginal. But I've often thought of guys I know who did grow up in the church—what an impossible thing it is the church asks of us all. I believe 100 percent that sex is best reserved for marriage, and that's God's design, but I can't get my head around that it was *his* plan that we wait ten to fifteen years in agony and angst."

I got married in my thirties, so I *completely* understand the agony and angst of waiting.

Sex is definitely pleasurable. And if the pleasure part is truly the main purpose of sex, then of course Amber and my coworker and much of our culture are right to believe it's unthinkable to marry someone with whom we haven't had sex. That kind of sex demands experience.

But the old fashioned way thinks about sex differently, more deeply and complexly. The old fashioned way acknowledges that sex is a wonderful, God-created, God-ordained gift to the human race. It is also something he created with definite, clear, and purposeful boundaries. He has reasons for wanting sex to be enjoyed within the safety of marriage.

Obviously there's the sexually transmitted disease argument. Another aspect is that engaging in sexual relations before marriage affects you mentally and emotionally. God desires for you and your mate to have a clean slate, with no sexual baggage or regrets. Sex is the most intimate part that you give to another person and that you receive from another person. But sex before marriage is counterfeit intimacy. It's more about instant gratification and self-serving pleasures than offering your body in unity and sacredness to another person.

In her article "Why I'm Still a Virgin at Age 26," Arleen Spenceley offers a great understanding of the importance of saving sex until marriage:

> The sex I save is rooted in chastity, which isn't the same as abstinence, but requires it until marriage. . . . Chastity is a

decision to die to self and to selflessly love (or to die trying). People who practice it regard all people as intrinsically valuable, reject their objectification, and uphold love as a choice in a culture that calls it a feeling.

Chastity shifts a person's focus from self to others, from what a potential husband could do for me to what he and I could do together—what we, as a unit, could contribute to the world. . . . For us, sex serves two purposes: procreation and unity. We don't believe we're supposed to decide to unite because sex is pleasurable, but to create a pleasurable sexual relationship with the person to whom we are permanently united. . . .

Maybe it's to a relationship's disadvantage to pick a partner with whom you're effortlessly sexually compatible over a partner who is willing to work through conflict. Maybe we do each other a disservice when we search for consistently gratifying sex but avoid opportunities to become people who can communicate when it isn't. Maybe how willing we are to practice and communicate, and to be uncomfortable and vulnerable in sex predicts how willing we'll be to do those things in other parts of a relationship.[2]

Practicing chastity gives us opportunities to practice other character traits that play out strongly in all aspects of marriage: patience, fidelity, compassion, and creativity. Chastity reminds us that marriage is about giving up our instant desires and sacrificing for the betterment of the other person—not so that we're always getting what we want out of it.

Ultimately, it isn't about saying no to sex right now; it's about saying yes to the freedom from guilt and sexual baggage, saying yes to understanding that love is often about dying to self, saying yes to a marriage bed that is pure.

God's will is for you to be holy, so stay away from all
sexual sin.

—I THESSALONIANS 4:3

CONSIDER THIS

If the idea of saving sex for marriage or that premarital sex is a
sin is brand new to you, take some time to think through God's
design for intimacy in marriage. Why do you think God created
sex to be between a husband and wife?

Read the following three Scripture verses. What does each
verse say about sex outside of marriage? Why do you think God
is so seriously against sex outside of marriage?

- "Why spill the water of your springs in the streets, having sex
  with just anyone?" —Proverbs 5:16
- "From the heart come evil thoughts, murder, adultery, all
  sexual immorality, theft, lying, and slander." —Matthew 15:19
- "Run from sexual sin! No other sin so clearly affects the
  body as this one does. For sexual immorality is a sin against
  your own body." —1 Corinthians 6:18

PUT IT INTO PRACTICE

Reclaim Chastity

If you have already given sex away, don't lose hope. Our God is a
God of forgiveness and second chances. Determine today to start
anew. Here are four ways to start:

1. **Acknowledge what you've done.** Premarital sex isn't a
   "mistake" or an "accident." According to God's Word, it is a
   sin (another old fashioned word). Rationalizing it does not
   remove the truth that it is a rebellious act against a holy
   God. Repentance means understanding the wrong you've

done, asking God to forgive you, and committing to live differently with God's help.

2. **Receive forgiveness.** The Bible tells us that God "has removed our sins as far from us as the east is from the west. . . . For he knows how weak we are; he remembers we are only dust" (Psalm 103:12, 14). When we accept forgiveness, we also can accept freedom from guilt.

3. **Reform your relationship.** With the physical part out of the picture, focus on building important relational skills that impact interactions outside the bedroom: communication, respect, goodness, kindness, integrity, selflessness, self-control, truthfulness. Reforming your relationship is achievable when you build it on God's ways.

4. **Find help and encouragement in community.** The more you lean on like-minded individuals within your church and friends and family, the stronger you can be to stay pure. Allow your community to hold you accountable, as you do the same for them.

the pleasure of purity

Purity does not mean crushing the instincts but having the instincts as servants and not the master of the spirit.

—ERIC LIDDELL, *THE DISCIPLINES OF THE CHRISTIAN LIFE*

"HAVE YOU READ *FIFTY SHADES OF GREY* YET?" an acquaintance asked me the other day.

"Um, no," I said, slowly. I wondered why she would ask me that question.

"I hear it's really good—kinky, but, you know, good. I may pick it up at the library. Everyone is reading it, so it can't be too terrible, right?"

Fifty Shades of Grey is a *New York Times* #1 bestseller, the story of a sadomasochistic billionaire, Christian Grey, who hires a young woman, Anastasia Steele, to work for him. Part of the deal is that she has to give him complete control of her life, including sexually.

The book sparked such a phenomenon that marketers scrambled to get in on the action. Adult bookstores had record-breaking sales. Companies made *Fifty Shades of Grey*–branded merchandise.[1] A hotel in England even replaced the Gideon Bible with the "soft-porn" reading material.[2]

What's the big deal with reading *Fifty Shades of Grey*? It's just a book, right?

When *Today's Christian Woman*'s blog ran a piece about the concern over people, especially Christians, reading this book, one commenter responded, "I find these books, personally, just an escape for a brief moment. They do not define who I am, where my marriage or my morals are and they certainly do not conflict with the relationship I have with our Heavenly Father."[3]

Unfortunately, as well-intentioned as this commenter is in her justification, she's wrong. The things we take in are the things that become part of us, our character. Jesus explained it this way: "It's not what goes into your body [meaning food] that defiles you; you are defiled by what comes from your heart. . . . For from within, out of a person's heart, come evil thoughts, sexual immorality, theft, murder, adultery, greed, wickedness, deceit, lustful desires, envy, slander, pride, and foolishness. All these vile things come from within; they are what defile you" (Mark 7:15, 21-23).

All sin begins with thought. That's why purity is so important to pursue.

Jesus was very serious about purity, about guarding our minds and hearts from those things that keep us from becoming the people God created us to be. In fact, Jesus also said, "You have heard the commandment that says, 'You must not commit adultery.' But I say, anyone who even looks at a woman with lust has already committed adultery with her in his heart" (Matthew 5:27-28). His antidote? "If your eye—even your good eye—causes you to lust, gouge it out and throw it away. It is better for you to lose one part of your body than for your whole body to be thrown into hell" (Matthew 5:29).

That certainly sounds as though God is serious about purity. He understands that the things we "take in"—whether it's movies, music, books, conversations, whatever—end up taking up residence within our minds.

Some people say purity is a different conversation among singles than it would be for married couples, but I don't agree. Being married doesn't mean you never struggle against impurity.[4] This isn't only about physical purity. It's about mental and spiritual purity.

I've found that's true about everything I take in through either my eyes or my ears. Those things become part of my thoughts, and eventually, if I'm not careful, they reshape my thought patterns.

In our culture it has become more and more difficult to keep ourselves pure from taking in those things that are not the best for us. Yet God calls us to pure hearts and minds—and to shut out those things that have dark, lingering effects on our brains and ultimately our character.

I realize I'm probably making this sound so easy. "Just do it. Just have pure thoughts." I know it isn't always easy! We have to remember that we're fighting a battle for our souls, and a lot of the battleground is in our minds. If you are truly struggling—maybe you have a problem with pornography or out-of-control thoughts—then I'm sure today's discussion can be overwhelming and guilt inducing. Please know you can find grace.

It takes work and commitment, but with God's help, you can retrain your brain. I want to be clear about something: having a thought that isn't God-honoring is not a sin; it's what we do with that thought that determines whether it grows into a sin or blows out the other side of our brain. When we entertain these thoughts, we open the door to impurity. When we acknowledge them and then refuse to allow them to take up residence in our brains, we are growing purity within us.

Although it's not easy, it is possible. What we think about matters. We can take captive our thoughts, and they can become our helpers as we allow the Holy Spirit to shape us. We can ask ourselves,

What would God want me to do? Would I think or fantasize about or say or act upon this particular thing if Jesus were physically present? Living intentionally—living the old fashioned way—begins with our thoughts. Once we realize that, together with Christ, we can be active participants in growing purity within ourselves, we will make enormous strides in becoming more like Christ and in growing character that draws people to us.

> Fix your thoughts on what is true, and honorable, and right, and pure, and lovely, and admirable. Think about things that are excellent and worthy of praise.
>
> —PHILIPPIANS 4:8

JOURNAL

Read these Scripture passages and write about what they mean to you, what God is saying in your life, and why you think it's important.

- "I made a covenant with my eyes not to look with lust at a young woman." —Job 31:1
- "Guard your heart above all else, for it determines the course of your life." —Proverbs 4:23; the NIV states it this way: "Above all else, guard your heart, for everything you do flows from it."
- "God blesses those whose hearts are pure, for they will see God." —Matthew 5:8
- Take captive every thought to make it obedient to Christ." —2 Corinthians 10:5, NIV
- "Let there be no sexual immorality, impurity, or greed among you. Such sins have no place among God's people. Obscene stories, foolish talk, and coarse jokes—these are not for you. Instead, let there be thankfulness to God. You can be sure

that no immoral, impure, or greedy person will inherit the Kingdom of Christ and of God." —Ephesians 5:3-5

CONSIDER THIS

1. How do I guard my mind from those things that shape my character in a negative way?
2. Are there things I have allowed myself to partake of that I justified by saying they don't define who I am?
3. Do I allow my thoughts to become fantasies and rationalize them because I'm not married yet and they aren't hurting anyone?
4. When I'm confronted with a situation or thought that conflicts with God's desires for me, how do I handle it? What are some ways I can handle it differently the next time I'm faced with a decision about purity?

a modest longing

Women are just like men; everyone wants it both ways.
—LUCKY CHUCKY, *OLD FASHIONED*

MY MOTHER HAS PLAYED A STRONG ROLE in my understanding of modesty: "You are not wearing that. No, don't even think about it. Go change. You're not a piece of meat for someone to gawk at."

But she's my mother, and mothers are kind of obnoxious about those things. Besides, clothing choices are sort of at a minimum—and modesty is not a hot trend right now. Plus, I'll be honest, after I lost thirty pounds, I wanted to show off my hard work. Sure, I was healthier, but really, I wanted to be a hottie! I wanted people to look at me and think, *Wow, what a great body*. It's a self-esteem builder. Shallow, of course, but still . . .

And this presents the dilemma: How do I practice modesty, which God praises in a person, and yet wind my way around it to build my self-esteem? I've tried to practice modesty all my life—mostly because of my mother, if I'm being honest. But besides my mother's continual voice ringing in my brain whenever I even look at something that shows off a little too much, I also carry two strong memories that play an even bigger role in my understanding of and quest for modesty.

The first is from many moons ago when I worked at a law firm in downtown Chicago. It was a Friday afternoon, and a paralegal stormed out of the elevator in front of my desk.

"I can't believe what that jerk attorney just said to me!" she said, her face fiery red. Before I could utter a word, she pushed on. "I mentioned to him that I was glad it was Friday and that I was going to have some fun with my friends at Blackies [a local bar]. And he said, 'Well, you're definitely dressed for it. Easy access.' *Easy access!*"

I glanced at what she was wearing: a fitted blouse that showed a bit of cleavage and a short, *short* skirt.

While the attorney *was* rude, he verbalized what others were probably thinking. I looked at her again. She looked good in her outfit. She had the body to carry it off. But it wasn't the wisest choice for her. I tucked that away in my brain: *Can wear, but is it the wisest?* And what is it saying about me if I do? Do I want other people to think, *Easy access?*

The other scene is from about a year ago. My dad and I were standing in line at IKEA, and the woman directly in front of us was wearing a shirt that showed off a rather generous amount of cleavage—I was afraid something was going to pop out. I've seen women dressed like that before, so I just rolled my eyes and didn't think too much about it. Until I saw my father's reaction.

He was embarrassed and struggling to figure out where to put his eyes. If he looked ahead in the line, there she was. He tried to stay turned toward me, but that was inconvenient since he had to keep turning around to move forward. My dad is a pure guy, and my heart ached that he was trying to remain pure by respectfully looking away—but it was tough to do. She was hanging out in full view, and there was nothing we could do about it.

It bothered me because this was *my dad*. And then it hit me, this is a *man*. This could be my husband struggling. What if by my clothing choices and actions I put someone else's husband or future husband in a tempting and potentially sinful situation? (We talked about lust and purity in the previous devotional.) Do I really want to play a part in that?

I realized anew that I need to watch what I wear and how I present myself, not only for my own dignity and self-worth, but because I can tempt others to fall into sin simply by what I'm wearing or by my actions (see 1 Corinthians 8:13).

In an earlier discussion (Day 13) we talked about emotional promiscuity. The ideal of modesty goes hand in hand with emotional purity. Modesty isn't just about what we wear; it's about our hearts. Do we wear a certain article of clothing or act in a certain provocative way to arouse desire? Beyond the sexual aspect, what about wearing extremely expensive designer clothing that arouses covetousness?

Modesty and accountability are important. As Paul tells us, women need "to be modest in their appearance. They should wear decent and appropriate clothing and not draw attention to themselves by the way they fix their hair or by wearing gold or pearls or expensive clothes. For women who claim to be devoted to God should make themselves attractive by the good things they do" (1 Timothy 2:9-10). Modesty applies to men, too. I've seen men who dress and act in such a way that tempts me to think impure thoughts.

Overemphasizing the physical cheapens a man just as much as it does a woman. We can make him into a "boy toy" when we focus on his abs and his amazing hairstyle and his sexy tight pants.

Modesty is really more than ensuring our necklines are high and skirt lengths low enough. Halee Gray Scott defines modesty this way: modesty is about becoming the "type of person who cannot imagine dressing any other way, because their hearts have been shaped toward virtue."[1]

We want to dress the way we want and yet insist that other people treat us with respect. As I quoted *Old Fashioned*'s Lucky Chucky previously, "Women are just like men; everyone wants it both ways." Most of us already know that men typically are sexually stimulated initially by visual cues. And studies are now showing that women are becoming more that way as well. So the truth is we can't have it both ways. Our choices tell others how to treat us—and that includes how we present ourselves. I'm not suggesting we don a burka or wear oversized clothes that take our choices to the extreme. We can still be confident and modest. It starts with attitude and internal issues and works itself out to the external.

Do I want to be a hottie? Yep, that base part of my human nature is still alive and well. But if I have to choose between being a hottie and possibly "cheapening" myself (as a male friend recently commented in regard to women's clothing styles) or being treated respectfully and taken seriously, then the latter wins out every time.

Turn my eyes from worthless things, and give me life through your word.
—PSALM 119:37

CONSIDER THIS

Closet Check

- Do a quick evaluation of your closet. What do the items there really say about you? Do they lead others to respond to you with respect and to acknowledge your value as a person created in the image of God? If not, when you wear them, what message are you presenting to others? Do your closet items present the possibility of making others envy you? Become aroused by you? What message do you want to send? How can you protect your and others' emotional purity?

- No need to pull out a ruler and measure the hem lengths of your clothing! But you may want to take inventory of your inner thoughts and self-worth. Taking clothing choices out of the picture, how are you building your character to become a person who longs after the desires of God? How does that affect your choices?
- Old fashioned attitudes about modesty could be pretty prudish and legalistic. In what ways can you incorporate the positive attributes of old fashioned modesty without becoming judgmental and harsh?

PRAYER

Lord, James tells us that if anyone lacks wisdom, we can ask you for it, and you will heap it upon us. I'm asking now for wisdom in how I present myself to others. Help me to remember that everything I do is a reflection of you and your living, breathing work in my life. Help me also to remember that how I present myself shows how much I honor and respect myself and how others view me. You value me; now may I value myself.

that's what friends are for

Fact. Most people know more about someone after a job interview for delivering pizzas than they do after most dates.

—CLAY, *OLD FASHIONED*

IN COLLEGE Dana (not her real name) started dating a guy who wasn't right for her. He wasn't a Christian and she was, so that was the first strike. He was rude to her friends. Second strike. And her friends noticed that Dana's personality started to change. No longer was she the exuberant, quick-witted girl everyone loved. Strike three.

After several months, a group of Dana's closest friends got together and confronted her about their concerns.

Nervous but determined, each girl laid out her observations. Dana listened quietly. At the end of the conversation, Dana said, "I really appreciate everything you've said, but you don't really know him like I do. You don't see things in him that I see. And ultimately, this isn't about you. I'm going to keep dating him."

Date him, she did. And then she married him. Then she walked away from her faith completely. After less than five years, she divorced him because "he was too controlling and I lost myself. I finally woke up."

Not all stories end like this, but many do. For Dana, the good news is that she is becoming more of her old self again. She's renewed her commitment to her faith. And she's dating a good man but "taking it slowly."

While I'm thrilled her life is getting back on track, I'm saddened by all the wasted years. She could have avoided so much pain and regret had she listened to her friends and believed they really did have her best interests in mind. They may not have seen things in him that she saw, as she told them, but they saw character traits more objectively. They saw the truth of who and what he was.

Why do we have such trouble sometimes believing our friends—at least where relationships are concerned? We'll trust them to fix our cars, recommend the best doctors or restaurants. We trust them more than we do our families, even. But then when they notice a red flag in a dating relationship, all of a sudden we think they have an IQ of 12—combined. They're blinded and don't understand. They don't get it. I think that's because we allow our emotions to guide us here (see Day 13 on emotional promiscuity).

God calls us to live in community. That's not because he's concerned that we'll be lonely. It's because he knows that we need trusted people around us who can keep us objective and who can warn us when we're headed in a wrong direction. Some life decisions are too important to make without consultation. Marriage is a biggie.

What God understands is that people tend to reveal more of themselves in group settings. How they interact with our friends shows bits of their true character. If they're rude to our friends, that's a core character flaw they have. And eventually, it will lash out against us.

I remember hearing an acquaintance tell me one time that a friend who hated her boyfriend was "just jealous because she doesn't have anyone right now." Okay, that may be the case. *However* . . . if she was so jealous she was trying to break up the relationship, then maybe the acquaintance needed to find a new friend. On the other hand, she may simply just not have meshed with the significant other. (I'm not a big fan of an acquaintance's husband, but because I see that he actually is really good for her, I suck it up and tolerate him.)

So I can understand why we may blow off one friend's judgment. If multiple friends are expressing concerns (even the tiniest ones), it benefits us to listen openly to their viewpoints. Friends tend to look more long range than we do. We see the ideal of the person; we're more forgiving of faults; we may even excuse certain behaviors that can end up being harmful to us.

God placed friends in our lives to help us navigate our life decisions. Good friends will encourage but will also do the hard work of admonishing and challenging. They love us with tough love.

The Quaker approach to this is fascinating. They call it collective leading. Professor and author Paul A. Lacey describes the importance of the community's aid in our decision making this way: "The private leading must be tested against the experience and collective leading of the worshipping community, not only to check the excesses of the willful or the mistaken, but also to give the support and strength of the religious community to what might otherwise be a lonely, ineffective witness."[1]

This is part of the old fashioned way—leaning into the wisdom and accountability of our community. Authentic community happens when people look out for one another, protect one another, and yes, even sometimes confront one another in love—as Dana's friends did.

If you're currently in a relationship (or when you get into one), trust your friends. Make sure that your potential beloved spends time with them. Let them ask probing questions—even as uncomfortable as it may be for you. Give them permission to do this, and thank them for looking out for you. They may see things objectively that you are unable to see. And it may well save your future.

Plans go wrong for lack of advice; many advisers bring success.
—PROVERBS 15:22

CONSIDER THIS

The Power and Purpose of Friends

The book of Proverbs has a lot to say about how our friends can benefit us as they evaluate our romantic relationships.

- "The godly give good advice to their friends." —Proverbs 12:26
- "A friend is always loyal." —Proverbs 17:17
- "There are 'friends' who destroy each other, but a real friend sticks closer than a brother." —Proverbs 18:24
- "As iron sharpens iron, so a friend sharpens a friend." —Proverbs 27:17

CONSIDER THIS

Ask yourself . . .

In the past, have my friends ever tried to warn me about a questionable relationship and I disregarded them? How did that turn out? Were my friends correct?

In what ways can I be more open to listening to my friends' perspectives?

PUT IT INTO PRACTICE

If your friends have never offered their opinions about your dating relationships, ask them to. Give them permission to share their honest thoughts. Make sure you listen honestly and openly and without feeling the need to defend yourself or the other person.

You don't have to respond or act on their opinions—especially if they're less than positive. Simply thank them for being honest, then contemplate their comments and pray for God to give you the discernment, wisdom, and knowledge to hear the truth and to act on it as God leads.

on accountability

Do you love this girl? Do you? If you do, life's too short. If you don't, life's too short.
   That's all I got for ya.

—GEORGE, *OLD FASHIONED*

SEVERAL YEARS AGO a close friend and I got honest with each other about the need to remain accountable in our marriages. We're both committed to our husbands, but we also realize how easily emotional connections can be made if we let our guard down even a little— especially since I interact with a lot of people because of my work. So we decided to tell each other about anyone we felt could potentially become an issue—though we didn't think we would ever participate in full-blown adultery, we wanted to make sure we're keeping our thoughts, words, and actions in check, that we're being faithful with our minds and words as well as our bodies.

So fairly regularly we will e-mail each other and ask, "How's it going?" We both know that means, "Are you keeping your pact? Are you guarding your mind, mouth, and actions?" We're sort of like AA sponsors for each other.

I was glad we had put that into place when an old junior high and high school flame contacted me on Facebook and started saying inappropriate things, such as sending me a quiz wondering how good a kisser I am. I sent him a "Watch it, buddy" response, and then because of my past with him, I contacted my friend and said, "Here's something that's going on. Not a problem for me, not interested in the least, but just wanted to let you know."

Honestly, it was easy because I wasn't interested *in the least*. But what if I were interested? What if he were a person who intrigued me or whom I knew I could become attracted to? Putting that accountability system in place adds a layer of protection so I can stay safe and helps ensure that I will succeed in my goals to remain pure.

If I arrogantly think I don't need anyone to hold me accountable, that I'm perfectly capable of handling temptation on my own, then I would open the door for sneaky, deceptive, innocent-appearing temptation to launch a full-out frontal assault. Knowing how fragile, how capable and ready for sin we are is such a protection for us.

The same is true for singles. When we think, *I'm an adult; I'm completely capable of handling temptation and safeguarding my character on my own*, we're inviting the enemy of our souls to test us with an, *Oh yeah? Try this and prove it!*

The same truth from yesterday's discussion on allowing friends to speak truth into our lives applies to today's discussion. It's not good for us to live in isolation and to try to stay virtuous alone. Our friends are in place to hold us accountable in keeping our virtue and purity intact.

I have a friend who helps me not eat carbs when I'm on a diet. Why would I then not have a friend to help me remain pure? Which is *much* more important than avoiding a bag of M&M'S (especially the ones with the pretzels in the middle).

Recently I was reading a blog post in which the author mentioned her newfound respect for Ashley Wilkes from *Gone with the Wind*.[1] It caught my attention because I always thought of Ashley as a spineless git. Love the movie; can't stand Ashley. The blog author wrote:

> After the war leaves them destitute, Scarlett approaches Ashley in order to lure him away from his wife and child. "Let's run away. . . . We can go to Mexico. . . . You know you don't love Melanie. There's nothing to keep us here." Unlike many men before him, Ashley resists Scarlett, telling her simply, "Nothing except honor. I love your courage and your stubbornness. So much that I could have forgotten the best wife a man ever had. But Scarlett, I'm not going to forget her."
>
> Ashley answers and resists temptation out of the strength of a virtuous character.[2]

Virtuous character? Really? He finally woke up when he realized the trouble he was in. That's not virtuous character; that's a virtuous *act*. There's a difference. Anyone can perform a virtuous act, even people with rotten character. If Ashley had had a virtuous character, he would have (1) put a stop to Scarlett's advances at the outset, (2) told a respected and trusted confidant that this could be a problem, and (3) avoided being alone with her. Ever.

We make decisions every day that we run by friends or people we trust. Living the old fashioned way allows us to understand deeply that we cannot live life in isolation and without accountability. We can try for a time, but we're guaranteed to fail.

And if you're nodding your head right now because you've blown it, take courage and have peace, my friend. Virtue can be reclaimed and restored. The old fashioned way is not only for those who have the appearance of perfection. As long as you have breath, you have the chance to make a U-turn or a redirection.

Just a brief caveat here. When we're talking about accountability, we're not talking about blurting out every sensitive secret. The unfortunate reality is that the nature of much of the evangelical church—times a hundred for those who make their living in it—doesn't necessarily breed this kind of environment. Even though in Acts and elsewhere it's clear that believers openly confessed sins (let alone temptations) to one another, when reputations and livelihoods are on the line and our personal testimonies and righteousness become our "currency," the need to appear "strong" is overwhelming. That's why it's important to find a *trusted* mentor or spiritual leader, someone you can trust who can keep confidences and hold you accountable.

If you don't have that person in your life, pray for one. God will provide. Keep your eyes open. That person may be someone you had never considered before.

Being old fashioned calls for us to be vulnerable with our mentors and trusted friends. And that's scary. But ultimately, it will keep us safe and protected.

Many who became believers confessed their sinful practices.
—ACTS 19:18

QUIZ

HOW VULNERABLE ARE YOU?

Take this self-assessment and see if you need to stretch yourself a bit more. Evaluate each statement with "Always," "Sometimes," or "Never."

1. I keep my temptations and failings secret.
2. I'm afraid to tell anyone about my temptations because I'm worried what they'll think of me, that they'll judge me.
3. I don't need to be accountable to anyone, because it's nobody's business what I do in the privacy of my life.

HOW DID YOU DO?

Here's how the Bible responds to each statement:

1. "Share each other's burdens, and in this way obey the law of Christ" (Galatians 6:2).
2. "Everyone has sinned; we all fall short of God's glorious standard" (Romans 3:23). "Let us think of ways to motivate one another to acts of love and good works" (Hebrews 10:24).
3. "Confess your sins to each other and pray for each other so that you may be healed" (James 5:16).

CONSIDER THIS

Choose Wisely

When seeking someone who can hold you accountable, it's best not to rush into a pact with just any person (friend or not). Here are a few questions to ask yourself.

- Is this person trustworthy? Can the person keep a confidence, or does he or she have loose lips?
- When I share deeply personal information, will the person listen without interrupting and without trying to fix?
- Does this person come off as judgmental? Or will he or she offer tough love with grace?
- Is this person supportive?

When you prayerfully choose your accountability partner, make sure to set clear guidelines for how and when you'll meet or connect. Then regularly evaluate how it's working and whether you need to make any changes. Communicate those clearly to your partner so you receive the most successful experience. Accountability isn't about control or taking advantage of someone's vulnerability. If the person you're trusting to hold you accountable misuses or breaks a confidence or begins to treat you judgmentally, then it's time to "break up" and find someone new. But if the person is honest—and you just don't like hearing the truth—pray about it and allow that person to hold your feet to the fire, knowing he or she is instrumental in helping to refine your character.

avoiding extremes

CLAY: Life isn't just all warm fuzzies.
AMBER: It isn't just all rules either. Religioso.

—*OLD FASHIONED*

EARLIER WE DISCUSSED THE OPTION of pursuing the old fashioned way of courtship (see Day 16), in which the strictest form allows for no physical touch and never being alone together without someone "chaperoning," in a sense. I encouraged you to consider this option for yourself, or at least parts of it.

So of course, I can see you coming to today's reading and thinking, *Are you kidding me? Avoiding extremes? Courtship feels pretty extreme!*

Sometimes, in Christian circles especially, we can get so caught up in rules that we miss the spirit of the law. We miss that the boundaries were set up for our protection and our good, not to make us miserable and prudish sourpusses. We can also overemphasize the physical boundaries so much that we turn a blind eye to other narcissistic relational behaviors.

Last year my husband and I traveled to the southwestern part of

Colorado to visit a friend, Rob. Rob works for the department of transportation. His responsibility is monitoring and maintaining the Million Dollar Highway, a scary stretch of road through the San Juan Mountains between Ouray and Silverton.

While we were visiting, he drove us over this pass. The drive is mile after mile of steep cliffs, narrow lanes, hairpin curves, and roads cut directly into the sides of the mountains. Now let's add to that an astonishing lack of guardrails and a white line for the edge of the road followed by a straight-to-the-bottom drop right at the edge of the white line. Finally, add to it a heavy snow that had started to fall.

"Why don't they put up guardrails?" I asked nervously, trying hard not to look down.

"Where would they put 'em?" Rob said and laughed. "You wouldn't believe how many cars and trucks come down this road, miss these curves, and go straight over the side."

"Oh, yeah?" I said. I felt ill.

"Yeah. But most of the drivers don't die, surprisingly enough. We get so much snow that it acts as a sort of cushion."

"So they don't die, but they have a heart attack on the way down. Pleasant."

Fortunately, God puts guardrails by every single cliff on our journey. If we lose our brakes and run wildly toward the edge, the guardrail is meant to save us—not to force us to lose out on the fun of careening over.

Being old fashioned is being a voice of reason in a world that rushes over the edge because they've removed the guardrails. We don't put our hearts in jeopardy, nor do we toy with the emotions of others.

So that explains the role of boundaries—but what do we do with them? For starters, we observe them, but we also understand that what might be a valuable boundary for one may not need to be a boundary for another. In other words, we avoid extremes—we avoid a set of rules for one person that also has to apply to everyone else.

Obviously God put in place nonnegotiable boundaries, but he left a lot of room for us to determine where the lines are. For some people, no kissing is a nonnegotiable. For others, it isn't. This isn't a one-size-fits-all list of rules. It's about getting our hearts in the right place and honoring everyone involved.

One side of the extremes pushes legalism. We create a set of rules that we expect everyone to adhere to. Clay needed to adhere to a stricter set of expectations because of how he had behaved in his past. That was an important line in the sand for him, which he refused to cross. But when he was tempted to the breaking point, Clay was forced to confront head-on the limits of his personal theories and the power of true grace and forgiveness. Extremes leave no room for such gifts. Instead, the legalistic extreme demands that we work harder to attain a certain level of righteousness and goodness. It demands conformity to law above all else. It's a works-based relational strategy.

Then when we think we're doing everything right, we can fall into the entitlement trap: God owes me. I've done everything right; now where's my happily ever after?

The other side of living in the extremes is to offer and live under cheap grace/cheap love, which argues that it doesn't really matter how we live. God wants us to be happy, so we can pursue that at whatever cost. God will forgive us.

Neither extreme is healthy or biblical. Instead, the old fashioned way allows us to have a balance. We have clear boundaries, but we also understand that we simply cannot reach a perfect state in our relationships. We are going to fail at some point. But when we do, God's grace covers us—not cheap grace, but God's grace that comes at a great cost, the cost of Christ's suffering and blood. When we're aware of that, our relationships become more intentional, our attitudes become more Christlike, and our actions provide healing and comfort in the midst of our brokenness.

We need the law; we need grace. Both work hand in hand to bring us the balance and joy our relationships so desperately need. Ecclesiastes 7:18 reminds us, "Pay attention to these instructions, for anyone who fears God will avoid both extremes." Another version says wisely, "Try to walk a middle course" because "those who fear God will succeed either way."

Search me, O God, and know my heart; test me and know my anxious thoughts. Point out anything in me that offends you, and lead me along the path of everlasting life.
—PSALM 139:23-24

CONSIDER THIS

- Do you struggle with extremes in some of your relationships or with yourself? If so, which extreme do you find yourself leaning more toward?
- What would taking a more balanced approach look like?
- Do you think God owes you something for your sexual purity? Or do you think God will punish you, or that you're unworthy of love, because of your sexual failures?
- The old fashioned way is about balance, intention, clear boundaries, and divine grace and mercy. Have you left any of those out of your life and relationships? If so, what would it take for you to say yes to trying that way of living?

PUT IT INTO PRACTICE

I've found these practices helpful to avoid extremes:

1. Spend time reading the Bible and looking, in particular, at the balance between justice and compassion that God applies to us.
2. Admit to the silly mistakes you have made in the past.

3. Let go of the things you cannot control, and focus on growing your mind and heart in the things that please God.
4. Spend time in silence and solitude, listening for and learning to discern God's voice.
5. Follow God's leading.

building good habits

We are what we repeatedly do. Excellence, then, is not an act, but a habit.
—ARISTOTLE

MY FRIEND HEIDI has the habit of expressing gratitude. She takes every opportunity to say thanks—even for the slightest thing. And I've noticed that I thoroughly enjoy being around her. Her face seems always to wear a smile. Her eyes crinkle with joy. She has a pleasant attitude—even when she's upset, she still seems calm. I think it's because of her outlook.

Tryon Edwards, an American theologian who lived in the 1800s, said, "Thoughts lead on to purposes; purposes go forth in action; actions form habits; habits decide character; and character fixes our destiny."

The psalmist suggests the benefits of forming good habits this way: "Oh, the joys of those who do not follow the advice of the wicked, or stand around with sinners, or join in with mockers. But they delight in the law of the LORD, meditating on it day and night."

They are forming a habit. And what happens when they form that habit? "They are like trees planted along the riverbank, bearing fruit each season. Their leaves never wither, and they prosper in all they do" (Psalm 1:1-3).

That stands true for my friend. Gratitude doesn't start with words; it starts with thoughts. And those thoughts lead her to act on them. After so many years, it has developed her character, and she expresses thanksgiving as easily as she says her name. And because of that, I've seen her thrive. That doesn't mean she never struggles or suffers. But her perspective on those struggles has helped her get through them in a healthy way and has strengthened her faith.

Ask any athlete about the power of forming habits. If you don't practice hard, you won't play hard. You won't have stamina to finish the game successfully. The same is true for relationships. We develop habits as single people that we take into marriage.

What are the habits you are developing?

Are they focused on spiritual practices or disciplines that draw you closer to Christ and make you more like him? Are they habits of criticizing and complaining?

Do they provide structure and a balanced rhythm of life to help facilitate your spiritual growth and maturity and to help protect and mentor others?

A benefit of creating good habits is that doing so puts you more in tune with learning God's will for your life. The apostle Paul says in Romans 12:2, "Don't copy the behavior and customs of this world [that is, don't make the world's habits your own], but let God transform you into a new person by changing the way you think. Then you will learn to know God's will for you, which is good and pleasing and perfect."

Habits help us live the old fashioned way. If you act with chivalry, for instance, and make a habit of opening the door for another person, when you enter marriage, you will carry that habit with you.

If you choose to say a prayer of thanksgiving before every meal, then you will carry that spiritual habit with you into marriage, which will help you to remain grateful for God's blessings over you and your family.

If you make a habit of paying off your debts every month, then you will carry that habit with you into marriage and avoid not only financial chaos but one of the top conflicts in marriage—arguments over money.

Discipline is difficult for a time; it asks us to sacrifice our natural, selfish will to something greater and holier. Diligently pursuing positive habits changes the way we relate to ourselves and others, and these positive habits ultimately glorify God.

It may be easy for us to be thankful when we receive a surprise check in the mail for a hundred dollars. But it takes discipline to be grateful when a child is born three months premature, or when we lose a job, or when our relationship with a family member gets strained. But the more we practice thankfulness, the more ingrained it becomes, until it takes over and eventually becomes our character.

The apostle Paul encourages us in our habits: "Whether you eat or drink, or whatever you do, do it all for the glory of God" (1 Corinthians 10:31). As you look toward the rest of this week, think about what habits you have formed—either intentionally (the good ones) or out of following cultural pressures (the bad ones). Which habits draw people (and a potential mate) to you? Which ones push people away?

Keep in mind the words of Paul: "All of you, slave and free both, were once held hostage in a sinful society. Then a huge sum was paid out for your ransom. So please don't, out of old habit, slip back into being or doing what everyone else tells you. Friends, stay where you were called to be. God is there. Hold the high ground with him at your side" (1 Corinthians 7:23-24, *The Message*).

Since Jesus went through everything you're going through and more, learn to think like him. Think of your sufferings as a weaning from that old sinful habit of always expecting to get your own way. Then you'll be able to live out your days free to pursue what God wants instead of being tyrannized by what you want.

—I PETER 4:1-2, *THE MESSAGE*

PUT IT INTO PRACTICE

What one habit would you like to form? Typically, it takes about twenty-one days to create a positive habit. Choose the habit you want to cultivate, then carve out time every day for a month to put it into practice.

At the end of the month, do a self-evaluation to determine how faithful you were and what the outcome is. How has it changed your outlook on life? How has it changed the way others relate to you or the way you relate to them?

CONSIDER THIS

In *Old Fashioned*, Clay tells Amber, "No one gets good at anything without practice. Everything I do now is preparing me for the kind of husband I'll be one day, God willing. Nothing magical happens when you walk down the aisle. Like it or not, what we do when we're single is what we'll do when we're married."

How are you preparing today for the kind of mate you desire to be?

DAY 27

how compatible are you?

Enough about me, let's talk about you. What do you think of me?
—C. C. BLOOM, *BEACHES*

KNOCK, KNOCK, KNOCK.

I glanced at the clock across my living room: 11:30 p.m.

Who in the world is knocking on my door at this hour? I muted the television and walked to the windows beside the door to peek out.

It was Jake (not his real name), the guy from my church I'd been casually dating for a month.

Immediately I opened the door. Something had to be up; this wasn't like him. As soon as I let him in, I could tell something was bothering him. He walked into the middle of my living room, turned on me, and in a tremulous voice said, "You're going to make me choose between you and my cat, aren't you?" He swayed slightly.

I blinked. "What are you talking about?"

"You're allergic to cats."

"Uh-huh. And?"

"And I'm going to have to give up my cat for you. I can see where this is going!" He started to cry.

I could see it too. Nowheresville. Really fast.

"Jake, trust me on this one, buddy. You are not going to have to give up your cat—or anything else—for me."

We stopped seeing each other after that. It could have been the crying over the cat that was the clincher. Or the fact that he went out with his friends and then came to my place at 11:30 at night, tipsy. Or that he pseudoworshiped his BMW, constantly fiddling with it, and kept the engine so clean you could eat off it (he told me so).

It could also be that we believed different things theologically. Or that I didn't like how his mother babied him. It's a toss-up.

What I do know for sure is that we weren't compatible.

He was handsome. He made a good living. He was smart. He was a Christian. And actually, even with the allergy, I liked his cat. But we weren't a good match for marriage.

One of the things I appreciate about many online dating services is that they attempt to help you figure out how well suited you are for each other before the physical or emotional aspects of a relationship get thrown into the mix and get everyone's priorities out of whack.

Some people think compatibility is that you like the same type of music, pizza toppings, and sports teams. Those are great things to connect over (after all, how could you *not* be attracted to someone who will belt out ABBA songs in the car with you?). But those things aren't really the essence of compatibility.

True compatibility is looking at the core beliefs we hold. Do they mesh?

For instance, does the person you're involved with feel strongly about the old fashioned values of integrity, trustworthiness, loyalty, self-control? Does that person save money or spend it like a fire sale is going on? Are his or her political views conservative while yours are liberal, or vice versa? Does he/she adore children, whereas your motto is children should be seen and not heard—and actually if they weren't seen either, that would be a double blessing?

In *Old Fashioned*, Clay and Amber started a compatibility quest early on when they began going through a book called *Red, Yellow, Green*. The premise of the book is that a couple would ask each other questions, and depending on the answer, they would mark *green* for move forward, this is good; *yellow* for proceed with caution, this may become a problem down the road; or *red* for slam on those brakes, this is a major issue that won't get better.

Why does it really matter? It matters because if there's one thing I can tell you with absolute certainty, it's this: when we're single, we can make a lot of exceptions and excuses over another person's character flaws or weaknesses. We can quiet our inner warnings (and sometimes outward warnings from friends and family), thinking, *But I can change this person after we're married.* Or as a friend told me before she got married, "My relationship is different. I don't set myself up for failure." (She and her husband of four years are now separated because of their incompatibility.) We believe the grass is greener on the other side. But I've been on both sides. I consider myself happily married, and I can say that the grass is exactly the same color on both sides of the fence.

Let's use conflict as an example. How do you argue? How does your beloved argue? Do you "fight" in a healthy way? How do you each handle family conflict?

I hear people say all the time that it doesn't matter so much because "love covers a multitude of sins."

Two words: *It. Matters.*

The biggest issue of compatibility is spiritual. I've heard all the arguments about "missionary dating." While it's purposely ambiguous in *Old Fashioned*, Clay and Amber certainly aren't on the same spiritual page when they begin their journey. Is that an issue?

I know people who have taken the missionary dating route and the other person converted, but these cases seem more the exception than the rule. I've known hundreds more who have taken that route and lost their faith. The risk—to your own soul—doesn't seem worth it. Obviously it's a decision that each couple has to make for themselves, but there are strong arguments against becoming romantically involved with a nonbeliever.

Paul warns believers, "Don't become partners with those who reject God. How can you make a partnership out of right and wrong? That's not partnership; that's war. Is light best friends with dark? Does Christ go strolling with the Devil? Do trust and mistrust hold hands? . . . Don't link up with those who will pollute you" (2 Corinthians 6:14-15, 17, *The Message*).

It isn't about love; it's about understanding. A nonbeliever can't really understand a believer. How *can* that person—when he or she doesn't know Jesus? When you face a challenge or struggle, you can't pray together or together study what the Bible has to say. And that chasm between you will pull you in ways you could never even imagine—all because you aren't connected spiritually.

This isn't about thinking that one of you is a better person than the other. The goal is to find someone who is headed in the same direction you're going.

This is not a police interrogation. I would not necessarily suggest that you rush to buy a book like *Red, Yellow, Green* and pull it out over dinner on your first date. But it is important to ask probing questions—and sooner rather than later. You want to hear answers while you still have a rational mind; in other words, before emotions and sexual tension dull your brain.

Be honest and say, "I don't want this to sound like a police interrogation, but I'm intrigued by you and want to know more about what makes you tick, about who you really are."

You don't have to ask every single question over the course of two hours. You don't have to pull out a notepad and take notes. And you definitely don't need a big guy to hold a bat and stand over the other person (unless, of course, your love interest doesn't like ABBA).

These are serious questions deserving serious answers, so make sure you provide a safe environment in which you can both respond. Decide beforehand what you're going to do if/when you hear an answer you don't like.

Actively listen, which means focusing on the other person's answers without thinking of your own responses. Let the other person finish before you respond to the answer. No interrupting. And don't be afraid to ask follow-up questions. You can let the other person know if you don't agree, but it's best to do so respectfully and with a willingness to understand and hear him or her out. One of the best ways to get someone to open up is to make that person feel heard, that you're genuinely interested and willing to consider that person's point of view.

And if the person gives vague, noncommittal answers—those are answers too, which might be an indication that you need to be cautious about proceeding in a relationship.

Later, when you're alone, make a list of those answers—in particular, the ones that caused concern. Hand them over to God, and ask him to give you direction. He will. "If you need wisdom, ask our generous God, and he will give it to you" (James 1:5).

Don't allow yourself to settle for less than the best. That may mean waiting longer. It may mean breaking off a relationship you know isn't right. It may mean standing up for yourself (maybe for the first time in your life) and believing that your core values never have to be compromised.

Red, yellow, green.

Be careful how you live. Don't live like fools, but like those who are wise.

—EPHESIANS 5:15

CONSIDER THIS

- Why do you think couples might not discuss compatibility issues with each other?
- Opposites attract. Why do you think that is? What can you learn from someone who is your opposite?
- What would be red flags of incompatibility for you?

redefining romance

Buy me flowers. Make me a card. I don't need you to make me your community service project. I need you to dance with me.

—AMBER, *OLD FASHIONED*

CHRISTINE WAS INVOLVED in a long-term relationship with Rob when she finally decided to break it off. I was surprised since they seemed like such a great fit for each other.

When I asked Christine for her reason, she said, "I don't know. I'm just still unhappy. He's a great guy, don't get me wrong. But he hasn't fulfilled me like I thought he would."

"What do you mean?"

She sighed. "I don't know. He's just not . . . romantic."

I thought she was crazy. She was going to break off her relationship with a man who was responsible, mature, trustworthy, genuine, a solid Christian, and who clearly adored her—all because he wasn't romantic?

"Wait a minute," I said, "didn't he buy you those flowers when you got that promotion? And he treats you like a princess."

"I know, but . . ."

I knew my friend well enough that I could see she wanted to say what she was really thinking but didn't want to sound harsh. I guessed she was ready to say, "He's boring."

"Seriously, Christine, you aren't going to find another guy like this. You can *teach* him to be romantic—however you define that. You can't teach someone to have quality character. This guy is a *keeper*."

I think Christine is like a lot of us. We say we want the good, kind, reliable person, but we really prefer the exciting, my-heart's-all-aflutter person. We have clear romantic expectations of what this person should do and be, and "usually pays the bills on time" isn't part of it. Somehow, the old fashioned qualities of kindness and reliability have become equated with "boring."

In *Old Fashioned*, Clay and Amber talk about the movie *Sleepless in Seattle*. Clay complains that he doesn't care for the movie because Bill Pullman's character is reliable and allergic to cats. He says the "boring guy with allergies always gets dumped in the movies, and it's not right, and it must be stopped. Am I boring?"

Amber replies, "In a good way."

And she's right! Clay isn't a romantic moron (as we see later in the movie); as a practitioner of the old fashioned way, he understands that romance is *bigger* than flowers and love poems. And Amber understands that too, ultimately. She wants the dancing under the moon, but she also wants the gentleness, goodness, and authenticity that come with it and say, *I'm dancing with you, and my heart is yours. I'm committed to you. I will respect and honor you when we're dancing and when we aren't.* Otherwise the dancing is nice exercise, but means little else when it's over.

The world knows how to do romance. It can package and sell it better than anything else. But look at the world realistically—is it a better place because of the kind of romance it sells? Does that kind of romance offer commitment, trust, spiritual connection? Or does it provide a nice but superficial diversion? Once the romance is over, is the relationship over too?

Like Clay says, "It's all icing, no cake." And it doesn't have to be that way.

Don't get me wrong, I'm a sucker for the kind of romance we see in movies and television. I swoon every time Rhett Butler carries Scarlett O'Hara up the stairs two at a time in *Gone with the Wind.* Just writing about it makes my toes tingle.

Jane Eyre, Romeo and Juliet, Wuthering Heights, Casablanca, The Notebook, Hallmark Movie Channel. Yep, love them all.

And I know it isn't just women who want to be romanced. Men want it too. Maybe it looks different; maybe it isn't an evening watching Meg Ryan and Tom Hanks films (unless you count *Courage Under Fire* and *Saving Private Ryan*). Maybe it's laughing at their jokes and making them feel special. Maybe it's cooking a favorite meal, or wearing nice clothes rather than the ratty sweat pants and Mickey Mouse shirt you've had since you were fifteen.

We all long for romance in some ways because it makes us feel special, important, desired. And who doesn't want that?

But framing romance only in the emotional context becomes dangerous when we buy into the idea that unless partners do "romance" right (as in an all-or-nothing ultimatum), they don't have the qualities that will keep a relationship strong. That simply isn't true, and it puts an oppressive burden on couples.

What would happen in our relationships if rather than idolizing how a relationship should be in the romance department, we painted a picture of what we really want our relationship to be—thinking about the character traits we long for in the other person? But one step further, think about what you bring to the relationship in terms of society's view of "romance" versus the old fashioned romantic ideal. Do you want to be doing everything "right" with that type of romance, yet failing in the areas that really count long term? Do you want your beloved to indulge in romantic poetry and dancing barefoot in the moonlight and taking you on picnics but not be committed to you or have a wandering eye or not be honest with you?

There's nothing wrong with the world's idea of romance. But it falls short—and that's the problem. Being old fashioned says, *I see your romantic ideal and raise it by two hundred.* In other words, old fashioned offers the flowers and the dancing and the love poems. But then it takes it beyond that to another level, which provides genuine commitment that never leaves, never betrays, never condemns.

It offers love.

> You are so handsome, my love, pleasing beyond words! The soft grass is our bed; fragrant cedar branches are the beams of our house, and pleasant smelling firs are the rafters.
>
> —SONG OF SONGS 1:16-17

CONSIDER THIS

- How would you describe your attitude toward romance?
- How do you define romance?
- What do you think is the difference between love and romance?
- How do you define the old fashioned ideals of romance?
- What would make one type of romance better than the other?
- Is a relationship about facing your lover, getting lost in each other's eyes, or about standing side by side, facing forward together?

PUT IT INTO PRACTICE

Want Some Real Romance?

Check out the Bible.

Yes, you can read that sentence again. In Song of Songs, Scripture offers a great perspective on romance between a man and a woman. Song of Songs is a series of poems celebrating and portraying romantic love between a husband and wife. It gets steamy, so perhaps keep the chocolate and oysters at bay.

in search of the perfect person

You don't believe there's a right person out there, for each of us? A soul mate?
—AMBER, *OLD FASHIONED*

I KNOW A WOMAN in her forties who has never been married. She's dated several men but always seems to find something wrong with them. She broke up with one man, for instance, because he stated that in marriage, couples could exhibit bodily functions (passing gas) in front of each other. She didn't agree. That was the end of that brief relationship.

One man's hair was too long. Another was too close to his friends. Another didn't belong to the same church denomination. Another wasn't romantic enough. Another wasn't interested in deep, soul-baring conversation every time they got together. And the list went on. She was never satisfied.

When we look for a person with whom we plan to share our life and love, we *should* have definite character traits we look for—steadfast nonnegotiables we can trust and be comfortable with. But too often we may become so picky about the "perfect" person that we overlook their many good qualities and home in on the traits that are different but not necessarily bad, allowing those qualities to become deal breakers.

We move into dangerous territory when we believe that another person can be "perfect" for us, that soul mate with whom we'll immediately connect, with whom we'll never argue, disagree, or become frustrated. Ask anyone who is or has been married, and they'll quickly tell you that perfection doesn't exist in marriage. Spouses—even soul mates!—let us down. Worse, we let down ourselves and our spouses.

Miscommunication, self-centeredness, pride, and innocent mistakes (which many mess-ups are) are part of every relationship. That's the secret power of relationships, though. They offer us grace for the times when the other person messes up—and for the many times when we fall short of our own standards.

When we set impossible-to-meet standards in our relationships (be they romantic relationships or with friends, coworkers, or family), we set ourselves up for certain failure. The statement has almost become cliché, but it's still true: "No one is perfect, no, not one."[1]

In the movie *Old Fashioned*, Clay sets such a high bar that no one can meet his expectations—not his friends, not other Christians, not even himself. So much of Clay's angst and disappointment comes because he believes that if he simply works hard enough, he can be perfect. And he expects others to follow his lead. He is let down over and over.

What Clay and so many of us fail to realize is that we can never reach that standard. No matter how hard we try or expect others to try, the bar is always just beyond reach.

Striving for and expecting perfection leads us to an empty, judgmental, harsh life. But mostly it leaves us lonely, never feeling settled, never satisfied, never fully able to know and be known.

When we're honest with ourselves, demanding perfection is often birthed out of our fears. We're afraid the other person will discover who we really are and will reject us, so we reject him or her first. Or we're afraid of being hurt or betrayed. Maybe it comes from watching someone you loved experience the pain of divorce, and you don't want to go through that. Maybe it's something you've experienced personally. Maybe someone violated you, and you refuse to become a victim again. So we respond by raising the bar so high that no one can ever reach it. No one can ever hurt us because no one can ever really know us. We don't allow for vulnerability or growth when we place that barrier in our relationships.

Longing for perfect relationships isn't a bad thing. Our Creator placed within us a yearning for perfection—because he is perfect and because it helps us put a proper perspective on our need for a Savior and our understanding of heaven. But demanding perfection of others and ourselves distorts the beauty of authentic relationships— the messiness that allows us to mature, to learn compassion and patience, to experience grace.

So what happens when the ideal crumbles? We gain the ability to walk into a relationship with others with open hands and hearts. We allow vulnerability and true authenticity to reside. We gain a perspective of who we can be.

Do we throw out our expectations and list of "definites"? No, not at all. There are nonnegotiables that we need to stand firm on. But we encounter freedom when we let some of the nitpicky things (and deep down, we know what they are!) slip by.

Perhaps when we set aside the ideal, the perfect person, understanding that it's okay for others to see our true selves as well, we begin to understand that *that* is where love actually begins.

By that one offering [Christ's sacrifice] he forever made perfect those who are being made holy.

—HEBREWS 10:14

QUIZ

Do You Expect Too Much?

Check any statements that apply to you. Be honest—this is about what you really think.

1. __ I believe there's one right person out there for me.
2. __ I believe that when I meet that person, we'll be happy and the relationship will be easy.
3. __ I believe that my soul mate will instinctively know what to do to meet my needs and desires.

If you answered yes to any of the above statements, don't beat yourself up. You're getting honest, and that's the first step to change. Ask God and your friends, family, or a mentor to help you discern what's really important and what expectations you can let go of.

CONSIDER THIS

- Do you hold high expectations out of fear? If so, what are those fears?
- What are some expectations that are nonnegotiables? What are some expectations that really don't matter?
- In what ways can you practice allowing others to see your vulnerability? Are there places in your life where you aren't authentic, where you're hiding? Why? What if you decided to let yourself make mistakes?
- What if the next time someone let you down, you offered grace? What do you think might happen?
- How do you view your relationship with God? How does that view impact what you expect or demand from others? From yourself?
- Read Hebrews 10:14 again. How does that apply to friendships and romantic relationships?

i think i love you

Love is the only gold.
—ALFRED, LORD TENNYSON

I LOVE WATCHING ROMANCE MOVIES. Girl meets guy. Drama ensues to throw them together. They fall in love. Awww.

And then I think, *Hey, wait a minute. That couple only knew each other for one week. How in the world can they be in love?* (Well, pretty much they can't, but falling in love in real time would be a very long movie to show.)

We live in a microwave society, where our food comes quickly, our texts are immediate, our Internet snaps to. That kind of immediacy has slipped into the way we view falling in love (or anything else that builds character). We even say, "I love you" too quickly and easily.

What does it even mean when we say, "I love you" to each other? To God? What does *love* really mean?

When I was dating my now-husband, it took him five years to utter those words to me. I was ready to say them within a month of dating him. When I expressed my frustration that he wasn't saying those words back to me, he told me, "I don't say those words lightly. They carry great weight to me. So I'll only say them when I'm ready to make a commitment to get married." (Can you imagine a movie *that* long?)

I wanted to base the relationship solely on my emotions toward him, but he had a broader view and understanding of what love really means.

What I discovered is that love doesn't really start until the person you're enamored of falls off his or her pedestal or you fall off the pedestal you're on and the illusion is shattered. The masks come off, the other person lets you down, or you realize how broken you both are. You're left with the imperfect, fallible human. And you stay.

That's the beginning of love. Not necessarily at the magical moment when we start exploring a new relationship and everything is fun and exciting. We're infatuated, maybe intoxicated by that other person. But even if we have complete integrity, there's going to come a moment when the scales fall off our eyes and minds.

What happens at *that* moment is where love kicks in. Do we do the hard thing and love the other person even when we don't feel like it? We act our love based on a decision, not a feeling. We commit to act lovingly.

We don't necessarily love them for their sake, but for ours. We can't love our enemies without that changing us (and believe me, when your beloved falls off the pedestal, they can definitely feel like an enemy!). We can't do the loving thing without being noble by the very act of doing it.

So many times I can look at my husband and have a profound sense of love wash over me. Yes, that's definitely love. But it's an easy love. The love that means the most, that is the "gold," as Alfred, Lord Tennyson, calls it, is the hard love. It's acting on behalf of someone else's best interest when I don't have warm fuzzy feelings about him or her. I don't always get it right, but I strive with every opportunity to become more and more loving.

In *Old Fashioned*, I think Clay understood this idea of love. He wanted to honor Amber and move slowly into a relationship with her. Yet I think Amber may have been the one to really grasp the depth and wonder of love's power when she told him, "I have a theory. Maybe love doesn't have to be perfect to still be worth it. And you don't have to be perfect for me to love you."

That's pursuing the old fashioned way: taking a sincere journey toward the heart of genuine and redemptive love. The Bible gives us a clear picture of this type of love. Over and over the writers remind us that love is offering genuine affection and honoring each other. Putting the other person's needs and desires before our own. Acting on the other's best behalf. (Do a word search of *love* in the Bible and see how often this type of love is discussed.)

If we want to understand the depth of that kind of love, all we have to do is look at Jesus. Singer/songwriter Chris Rice explains it this way: "Sometimes love has to drive the nail into its own hand. . . . The love Jesus asks us to show is the kind He showed us—the kind that means sacrifice, not just feeling good about someone. Love is costly, and the highest love costs the most."[1]

> There is no greater love than to lay down one's life for one's friends.
>
> —JOHN 15:13

CONSIDER THIS

- How do you define love? Love for God? Love for your beloved? Love for others?
- What if your favorite thing about your beloved (looks, intelligence, humor) was taken away: What would love look like then?

- Here's the toughest call of true love: "Husbands must love your wives with the same love Christ showed the church. He gave up his life for her" (Ephesians 5:25). Christ died for the church. *That*'s love.

CONSIDER THIS

Love Check

Living out love is a noble and high charge. Read through 1 Corinthians 13:4-7. Remove the word *love* and replace it with *I*. See how many of these are true for you and how many you need to still work toward.

I am patient and kind.
I am not jealous or boastful or proud or rude.
I do not demand my own way.
I am not irritable, and *I* keep no record of being wronged.
I do not rejoice about injustice but rejoice whenever the truth wins out.
I never give up, never lose faith, am always hopeful, and endure through every circumstance.[2]

PRAYER

Wow, God. I didn't do so well on the self-evaluation. I do some of those things, but I really struggle to do all of them all the time. I fall so short of your perfect standard of love. But thank you that you don't. You don't have to practice love, because you *are* love. Help me to remember that love is a journey I grow in. Thank you for offering your loving mercy when I fail. I don't have to feel overwhelmed by guilt and despair because I fall short of the love described in 1 Corinthians 13. And help me to take seriously what love is so that I don't confuse the feeling of infatuation with the deep, rich love that stands strong in the midst of trouble.

a word to the men

Treat a man as he is, and he will remain as he is. Treat a man as he could be, and he will become what he should be.

—GOETHE

I USED TO WORK WITH A MAN who was the sweetest, most gentle person. He fell in love with this young woman who broke his heart. (Read: pulled it out of his chest, got into her car, backed up over his heart, and hit it again about a dozen times.) He went from being a noble, virtuous man to becoming the most promiscuous person I'd ever met. He was bound and determined not to get hurt again, so he became a user.

So when I encountered Lucky Chucky in *Old Fashioned*, I couldn't help but think of my former coworker.

The cliché goes, "Behind every cynic is just a wounded romantic." Hurt people hurt people. When discussing Lucky Chucky, even his friend Clay says, "He's a victim."

This is especially devastating when we have a prideful righteousness issue: the more we think God owes us something, the worse this kind of thing can go.

When a man loves a woman—as the song goes—he gives her incredible power to make or break him. And if he doesn't have his character firmly cemented in his identity in Christ, when heartache comes, it can destroy something that God holds as priceless.

So I want to encourage you.

First off, I want to give you credit for opening your mind to the possibility of living according to old fashioned values. Just picking up this book is a great step toward trying a "new" and different way.

Second, I want to acknowledge something I feel saddened about for you: often—especially in the church—men have gotten the raw end of the relationship deal. We tend to point out all the things men do wrong, rather than starting with the basic assumption that men are capable of doing things right. I've heard numerous messages from sermons, books, and radio preachers that pound the importance of virtue and then judge men for being the ones who stalk, prey upon, and steal a woman's purity and innocence. Even in the "good old days," that assumption wasn't necessarily true. Women can sometimes be better instigators, manipulators, and players than men!

On a more gentle note, it's difficult for Christian women at times because they want to be desired (that's natural), and so they often send mixed signals to guys. The woman wants to be wanted, but she wants the man to control himself—but not too much. It's all a little tricky!

So I want to talk with you from the perspective of believing that you want to live a life that honors God, yourself, and others. Maybe you're not sure how best to do that. Maybe you've never seen it modeled. Maybe you've tried and messed up and think it may be hopeless. Maybe you've worked hard to live that way and a woman you were involved with pushed you to break some boundaries that you held.

Wherever you find yourself, you can start fresh. One of my favorite traits about God is that he exudes mercy: "His mercies begin afresh each morning" (Lamentations 3:23). In other words, today is a new day. If you've hurt someone or have been hurt by someone, you don't have to allow that to keep you from living a Christlike life.

Part of it is understanding who you are—as a *person* created in God's image, and beyond that, as a *man*. It takes a lot of courage to grow in the face of scrutiny.

Our culture still has a little (not much) residual admiration for purity or virginity in women. In men, it's a sign of weakness: there *must* be something wrong with you. Young Christian men need affirmation in their masculinity when they show restraint and respect for young women.

As you grow in the knowledge of who you are created to be, you will begin to display more confidently those character traits that will draw people to you for the right reasons. You'll be better able to discern who is the right person for you to allow close and who are the people you need to stay away from.

That's a tough road—especially since our culture and even the church don't give you much encouragement or direction.

In the blog post "Why Young Men Aren't Manning Up," Jonathan Sprowl explains it this way:

> The path to responsible manhood is not easy and staying
> a boy is. Battling Captain Hook with the Lost Boys
> (or playing hours of Call of Duty) is thrilling. Taking on
> a mortgage and responsibility for the livelihood of others
> is frightening. If the modern world is beating him down,
> at least he can be the hero of his own fantasy world. Judging
> by portrayals of men in the popular media, they don't
> expect much of him anyway.[1]

So what's the best way to learn about old fashioned values and to incorporate them into your life? Again, I'll let Jonathan speak to that (since he's a guy and has earned the right to say it better than I could!):

> The key to our salvation is breaking the cycle. We humans learn by example. Young men have been cut adrift to carve out a path for themselves with only the media to guide them. The past decades have seen older women blazing trails for younger women and bestowing them with a sense of legacy. Men need other men to exemplify masculinity: a robust, noble, responsible masculinity. Older, wiser men must walk beside younger men in a Titus 2:6-7 manner, encouraging them to show integrity and self-control.

Find a mentor who can guide you and help you build wisdom and discernment in your relationships. Ask God to bring one into your life, if you don't have one and don't know where to look. Ask a pastor or trusted coworkers if they can recommend anyone. And listen to the still, small voice of your conscience leading you.

One of the best mentors you can have? Jesus. Read the Gospels in the Bible (Matthew, Mark, Luke, and John), and watch how Jesus treated other people.

"I know that his story has been hijacked to promote whatever version of masculinity is in vogue to the point that our vision of him is schizophrenic," says Jonathan Sprowl. "But I also believe that men who are patient enough to hear what he said and dedicate themselves to following him will find no greater example of what it means to be a man."

And may Christ's example urge you on to continue growing into the man God has created you to be.

> Encourage the young men to live wisely. And you yourself must be an example to them by doing good works of

every kind. Let everything you do reflect the integrity and seriousness of your teaching.

—TITUS 2:6-7

CONSIDER THIS

- What are my motives when I date a woman? Are they pure—seeking to honor her virtue and lead the relationship in a way that will bring out the best in both of us?
- Do I have someone to whom I can make myself accountable to grow spiritually? Do I have a more mature man in my life who will help me make the right decisions about how I treat others?
- If I don't, what are some steps I can take to find that person and begin the process of strengthening my character?
- What does today's culture call men to be? Do I agree with this picture or not?

a word to the women

We are women, and my plea is, Let me be a woman, holy through and through,
asking for nothing but what God wants to give me, receiving with both hands
and with all my heart whatever that is.

—ELISABETH ELLIOT

WHEN I WAS DATING my now-husband, he said something to me that
no one had ever said before: "You have a meekness about you that's
really attractive."

Huh?

I wasn't sure if I should thank him or slug him.

I'd heard men tell me I was pretty and fun to be with, but no one
ever mentioned that I was meek. I wasn't sure what it even meant.
Although it sounded spiritual ("Blessed are the meek: for they shall
inherit the earth," Matthew 5:5, KJV), it also sounded a lot like the
word *weak*. And I didn't like that. At all.

I had—and still have—no interest in being an old fashioned
girl in the negative sense of the word. You know, the mentality that
women are second-class citizens, "fragile" creatures who need a man
to take care of them because they can't possibly survive without one.

(Picture a woman placing the back of her hand against her forehead and swooning, "Oh, my!") That was my mental image—quite wrongly—of what *meek* meant before he mentioned it and before I spent time really considering the biblical definition of it.

Meekness is the ability to show a quiet, kind, humble, and mild strength of character.

Once I grasped it, I thought, *This is who Jesus is. He was considered meek.*[1] *So it must not be a bad thing. Scott was actually complimenting me.*

He was telling me that I had a gentle and mild spirit. He saw a character trait in me that I hadn't really seen in myself. And that made me want to be that way—not just with him but with others. Once he verbalized that to me, something within me changed. I really worked at being a softer, gentler person. I admit I fail more often than I'd like, but it made me realize that being meek isn't the same as being weak. He didn't try to change me; he wanted to bring out the best in me.

And in return, I sought to bring out the best in him. I realized that I could focus on his positive attributes and encourage him in those (including *his* meekness).

If I've learned anything on this life journey in regard to how our character affects our relationships, it's this:

(1) As women we don't often give ourselves credit for the ways God has gifted and created us. Our insecurities can overwhelm us at times, and we work to protect ourselves from being hurt or from being taken advantage of. But God created us as women, not men. It's okay for us to be different, to embrace the softer, more nurturing side of God's character. That isn't a sign of weakness. That's something to be celebrated.

(2) Women have incredible power to build up or crush men—and it's easier than we'd believe. As women we understand how deeply insecure we can feel. But we neglect to understand how deeply insecure men can be too. One caustic remark that shows disrespect can wound like nothing else. Nagging, belittling, controlling. None are attractive; all will push a person away.

Marlene Dietrich, a famous actress whose heyday was in the 1930s, said, "Most women set out to try to change a man, and when they have changed him, they don't like him."

God has placed in our hands the power to build up or tear down a man. How we choose to use it determines how successful our relationships will be.

According to an unscientific study I did with about a dozen men I know, men have two basic emotional needs: to feel respected and to feel competent. So how do we use that information for good?

In a blog post, "Why Young Men Aren't Manning Up," author Jonathan Sprowl suggests this:

What can women do to help [men]? It starts with being part of the solution and not the problem. As tempting as it may be, resist the temptation to join the man-bashing bandwagon.

Even when said sarcastically, these remarks undermine attempts of young men to put themselves together and reinforce the stigmas attached to them. Sure, maybe he dresses like a bachelor and cooks like a bachelor, but at least he's putting forth an effort (if he really is).

On the positive side, encourage winsome qualities in him. When he shows initiative, point it out. Depending on the depth of your relationship with him, when he's dropping the ball, lovingly let him know, and give him a chance to fix things.[2]

More than anything else, our responsibility as women isn't to change men; it's to become more Christlike ourselves. Let God be God in a person's life. Let the Holy Spirit guide you. Trust that God really is working behind the scenes in your life and in the lives of others. And keep your focus on the prize of becoming the person God created you to be. If you do this, the other pieces will fall into place.

> I don't mean to say that I have already achieved these things or that I have already reached perfection. But I press on to possess that perfection for which Christ Jesus first possessed me.
>
> —PHILIPPIANS 3:12

CONSIDER THIS

- How do you treat others, particularly men? Do you ever participate in man bashing? If so, even in jest, why?
- What are some ways you can build into a man's character and offer him respect and dignity?
- Do you ever struggle with accepting who God made you to be? Why is that? What would it take for you to believe in yourself and God's gifts to you?

JOURNAL

- Write about what being meek means to you. Is that something you would aspire to? Why or why not?
- In what ways was Jesus meek? How can you best follow his example?
- In *Literature in My Time*, author Compton Mackenzie writes, "Women do not find it difficult nowadays to behave like men, but they often find it extremely difficult to behave like gentlemen." What do you think the author meant by that statement? Do you find areas in your life where this is true? If so, write about how you can be more aware of that and why it's important.

the purpose of marriage

Nothing magical happens when you walk down the aisle. Like it or not, what we do when we're single is what we'll do when we're married.

—CLAY, *OLD FASHIONED*

A FEW MONTHS AGO my husband and I were having supper with some friends, and the conversation moved to marriage. The wife made the comment, "We don't know any married couple who is happy." Then she looked at me and said, "Are you two happy?"

That was terrible timing, because right before we met them at the restaurant, my husband and I had gotten into an argument.

Everything within me wanted to say, "Well, of course we're happy. We couldn't be happier! I love being married. It's just super swell!"

But instead, while my husband took an intense interest in studying the tines on his fork, I spoke the truth: "No, actually, not right at the moment. In fact, I'd like to drop him off about twenty-five miles out of town and let him walk home. In the rain. Without his cell phone."

Our friends laughed. They know we can be brutally honest about such things. And even though my husband and I didn't like each other at that particular moment, I knew we were okay. We weren't going anywhere; we've made a covenant to do life together no matter what, no matter how we feel. Period.

This was a bump in the road. And that was the perspective we needed to keep. I'm not happy in my marriage every moment of every day. And neither is my husband. But we both realize that ultimately marriage isn't about making each other happy. That's a nice benefit, but it isn't the goal. The goal, as Gary Thomas so eloquently states in his bestselling book *Sacred Marriage*, is to make us holy.

How can marriage make us holy? By making it harder to hide, by exposing our sin, by providing opportunities to serve, by . . . (fill in the blank, and you've got it).

That puts marriage into a different category. No longer is it a deal or a contract (you do this; I do that—as long as we keep the agreement, we stay married). It's a covenant. Some even call it a sacrament. This covenant says, "I vow to experience life with you, to love you (not a love based on feelings, because those can ebb and flow, but a love that is a decision beyond any emotion). I will do everything in my power to seek your best and to fully live out 1 Corinthians 13. I will remain faithful to you, as God is my witness."

That's a serious vow. In fact, when Jesus talked about marriage, his disciples were so stunned by the reality of the covenant that they said, "If this is the case, it is better not to marry!" (Matthew 19:10).

Marriage is a huge step of faith into the unknowable. But once you make that commitment, love has a firm place to grow.

When I was single, marriage looked so simple. *What's the big deal? My marriage won't have the kind of struggles these other marriages have.* And then I got married.

The living together part isn't the problem. The mirror my husband holds that reflects my soul and my character is what causes the discomfort. One of the purposes of marriage is to grow us into the likeness of Christ—I'd say it's the best and most successful way, if we allow it. It's also the most painful.

In marriage I have no place to hide my sin. At some point the carefully constructed facade that I carry around for the world to see has to come down, and my spouse is there to see the real me and to call me out on my weaknesses and flaws. God designed it that way in order for my spouse to be an instrument to mature me and for me to mature my spouse. In a sense marriage is like a refiner's fire; you go through the heat to come out pure.

When you're willing and malleable and humble, the mirror and the fire force you to repent because someone's up in your business, and this exposes more sin in you. You can repent of that sin, and in the process both of you become not only closer to each other but closer to Christ.

It isn't that I couldn't mature as a single person. It's simply that as a single, I didn't have as many people pressing in on me, so it was easier to ignore my sin until it could fester and get worse. To be fair, I know a lot of couples who don't deal straight with their sin. Even in marriage, they withdraw, go to their corners, give the silent treatment, pretend that nothing is wrong. That will last only so long before the potential for greater sin and possibly divorce sets in. That is not what God had in mind. Marriage is *supposed* to be difficult and at times downright painful. That's part of maturing.

Marriage doesn't guarantee happiness. It doesn't guarantee spiritual maturity. It's what you choose to do with marriage that determines the depth of God's work in your life. If you don't work through the difficult parts, your spouse will continue to rub up against those flaws of yours like a shoe rubs against a blister.

The old fashioned way understands that marriage is intended to grow you—it's about sacrifice, laying down your life daily. It's a chance to serve each other and together to serve a world in need.

Courtship isn't really about finding someone to meet all your needs—only God is capable of doing that. Courtship and then marriage are really much more about growing you into a servant, shaping your character so that you become less about you and more about the other person. While marriage offers the promise of companionship and joy, it's much more about stretching and growing you into someone who becomes like Jesus. The expectations we place on our significant others (keep me from being lonely, be my friend, make me happy)—those are not bad expectations to have. But we need to understand that no person will be able to satisfy those expectations 100 percent of the time. Only God can do that.

Often we place the longing we have for our spiritual completion (God) on another person, which that person was never created to fill. When we do that, we inevitably discover that our expectations of that other person fall short.

The good news of this old fashioned message is that as you stick your relationship out, as you *act* loving toward each other, then the practice of doing those things will ennoble you in the process.

> Give honor to marriage, and remain faithful to one another in marriage.
> —HEBREWS 13:4

CONSIDER THIS

- What do you think about the idea of marriage being a covenant?
- Do you agree with the statement "By growing closer to someone, more of your sinfulness is revealed, and this can draw you closer to God"? Why or why not? How have you seen this work itself out in the married couples you know?
- "We need a witness to our lives. There's a billion people on the planet. . . . I mean, what does any one life really mean?

But in a marriage, you're promising to care about everything. The good things, the bad things, the terrible things, the mundane things ... all of it, all the time, every day. You're saying, 'Your life will not go unnoticed because I will notice it. Your life will not go unwitnessed because I will be your witness.'" How does this quote (from the movie *Shall We Dance?*) apply to what we've discussed in today's reading?

- What does serving look like to you? How does the attitude and approach of "This is my chance to serve you" change everything?
- In what ways are you preparing yourself now to be married?

PUT IT INTO PRACTICE

Rik Swartzwelder, the writer and director of *Old Fashioned*, says, "If there's anything I know about marriage it's this: it is much harder when you're in it than it appears like it should be from the outside." Have you ever expressed that same idea? Take some time this week to talk to a few married couples who seem like they have a strong marriage. Ask them about this statement. Then ask them to share honestly with you what they've found to be true about marriage and what it has done for their character.

how do i know?

CLAY: How did you . . . know?
GEORGE: Know what?
CLAY: Know.
GEORGE: Know? Know. Good question.

—*OLD FASHIONED*

IN *OLD FASHIONED*, Clay asks an antiques peddler, George, the all-important question about marriage: "How did you know?" Clay was saying in essence, "How did you know your wife was the right person for you? I want a guarantee that the decision I'm making is the correct one."

Oh, if only marriage offered a guarantee! But how do you guarantee a lifetime of happiness and commitment and friendship when you're talking about a relationship between two broken people? No one enters marriage perfect. We're all fallen human beings.

That's why marriage is a covenant and not a contract. A covenant reminds us that as broken people we will mess up (that's the guarantee!), but it calls us to remain steadfast despite our foibles.

I've been asked the "how did you know?" question multiple times by single women. And I'll tell you what I tell them.

I knew during our first official date, which was about two months or so after we met. We were walking through Chicago's O'Hare Airport (this was pre–September 11, when you could go to the gates without a ticket) and basically interrogating each other (politely, of course), and it hit me: *I'm going to marry this guy.*

And that's when I started to hyperventilate.

That didn't mean for the rest of the time we dated I never had doubts. I watched his character and the way he treated me and others. I prayed. I talked to spiritual mentors. But at the proverbial end of the day, ultimately it came down to my decision and commitment.

In my mind, once I made the vow to him, it no longer mattered whether "I knew" or not. I had to trust going into the marriage that I had done my homework, that I had vetted this guy, that I was entering a covenant with my eyes wide open.

I think this is what I find so intriguing about George's character in *Old Fashioned.* He had dated his now-wife and liked her okay, but only kept dating her because he never knew how to break up with her (no time ever seemed right), then he ended up marrying her, and stayed married to her. Once he had married her, he stayed because of his old fashioned values and his understanding of the sacredness of marriage. Out of that commitment, love grew.

It reminds me of the scene in *Fiddler on the Roof* where Tevye asks his wife, Golde, "Do you love me?"

Golde sings, "For twenty-five years I've lived with him, fought him, starved with him. Twenty-five years my bed is his. If that's not love, what is?"

"Then you love me?" Tevye persists.

"I suppose I do," Golde finally responds.

"And I suppose I love you too."

Sometimes we want to know if the other person is "the one" because we're looking for that illusion or that thing that's perfect, and when the feeling pales or everything isn't easy and comfortable, we question whether or not we're making the right choice.

For George, he wanted to break up but never found the right time; then his relationship took on its own momentum, and after so much time went by and he finally had the perfect moment to break up, it slowly dawned on him: *Wait. I do love her.* For whatever reason, George got married. And as he stuck his marriage out, a quiet love grew.

Love is ultimately an act of the will more than it is a feeling. As we act lovingly toward another person, the feeling of love will grow simply by the action of loving.

To be honest, you may never have an absolute guarantee that this is the person you are supposed to marry. But there are some ways you can help discern your relationship and its future.

- *Don't rush it.* This especially becomes an issue the older we get. We hear the clock ticking, and we think this may be our last opportunity, so we settle for Mr. He'll Do/Miss She'll Do instead of holding to a higher standard. (We'll talk about waiting in an upcoming reading.)
- *Pray.* Prayer isn't simply uttering, "God, send me somebody!" or "Is this the right person for me?" Prayer is listening. Get away from anyone or anything that distracts you from hearing God whisper into your soul, and spend some time in silence. It will clear your heart so that as God directs, you'll be more aware of his leading.
- *Talk with your friends and spiritual mentors.* Ask for their honest insight and then listen as they speak. Don't try to defend your choices. Instead, let their words soak in, knowing they love you and want what's best for you. Then take their advice to God, too, and ask him to help you determine what's

the golden advice you need to heed and what isn't. (See Day 23 for more on this topic.)

- *Ask yourself some simple questions.* The biggest one is, "Does this person share my spiritual beliefs and values?" (We discussed this briefly in Day 27's reading.) If the answer is no, your direction is clear. In 2 Corinthians 6:14, Paul warns believers, "Don't team up with those who are unbelievers. How can righteousness be a partner with wickedness? How can light live with darkness?" No amount of rationalizing ("But he respects my faith" or "She's spiritual; she just isn't religious") will change the truth of "Not the one."

If a person is perfect on paper but somehow manages consistently to make you feel bad about yourself, that person is likely not the best match for you.

If you at least start with these action points, you will have a clearer direction and understanding of who you are, what you want, and whether the other person fits with you in the best possible way.

> I am giving you a new commandment: Love each other. Just as I have loved you, you should love each other.
> —JOHN 13:34

PRAYER

God, my mind is filled with so many questions. I'm afraid of making a decision I will regret. And I know that marriage is one of the most important decisions I will ever make. I know there are no guarantees in this life, but I trust that you will give me discernment and wisdom to choose wisely. Thank you.

breaking up is hard to do

*The most important human endeavor is the striving for morality in our actions.
Our inner balance and even our very existence depend on it. Only morality
in our actions can give beauty and dignity to life.*

—ALBERT EINSTEIN

A FEW YEARS AGO a friend of mine was having lunch with some people
at a restaurant in Florida when they began to talk about the concept
of breaking up.

"We were talking about how there's never a convenient time to
break up with someone," he told me. "There's always going to be a
reason why you shouldn't. Right? And then you're, I don't know, *stuck*."

I don't care what anybody says, breaking off a relationship is a
terribly difficult thing to do—especially if you've invested anything
emotionally into that other person.

But there may come a time when you get a certain distance into
the journey and realize the relationship isn't growing or going in the
right direction. And it's time to end it.

We don't pursue the old fashioned way only in growing our
relationships, but also in ending others. This is the time when it's

175

especially important to bring out the best of your character, whether you're ending it or the other person is.

I know a lot of us want to avoid doing the hard thing, so we prolong it. But that doesn't make it easier. Honesty is important.

I used to work at a place where they had a number of layoffs. Each time, instead of doing the deed quickly and getting the pain over with, the executives would linger and procrastinate. My coworkers and I joked harshly that it was the difference between being put in a guillotine that uses a sharp blade or one using a butter knife.

Our human nature is fragile, and as we open ourselves to becoming vulnerable (even slightly) emotionally, we need to treat the ending quickly but delicately. It's important to remember that each person has an inborn worth and is precious to God. That means they deserve being treated with dignity and respect. It's that "I" and "Thou" mentality of valuing the other again. God delights in us when we take intentional and relational responsibility. So if you know a relationship is a no, then you are morally obligated to stop tugging on the heartstrings.

This, too, is part of our maturing experience. And God requires that in all our relationships, even the ending of them, we must act out of love for the other person.

Samuel Ullman, an American poet and humanitarian, said, "Maturity is the ability to think, speak, and act your feelings within the bounds of dignity."

When I was fresh out of college, I was involved in a serious relationship that I knew wasn't the right one for me. But because I hate conflict, I avoided the inevitable conversation to end it. Instead, I continued in the relationship and grew bitter and mean toward the other person. That was my fault, not his. I could have been honest and saved us both so much emotional damage. But I wasn't. And when it did finally end, I was harsh and hurt his dignity. That's an intensely painful regret that I carry. I've since sought forgiveness, but how much better it would have been had I handled the situation with spiritual maturity, following the old fashioned ideals of kindness and virtue in my dealings.

"Shoulda, coulda, woulda" does me no good. It does no one any good. There is an immense difference between being harsh and being firm.

We can do the right thing. We can ask God to show us the right time and then act. We can use our words firmly, but as a healing balm to save someone's dignity. We may not like the other person, but we still are called to love them and to remember that Jesus died for them and that God desires good things for the other person too.

And if you're the person who has been dumped, regardless of how the dumper treated you, God still calls you to show maturity and grace in your dealings with and in how you talk about that person. No gossip, no hurtful words to cover over your own pain. That will ensure when you look back, you'll have no regrets about the way you handled it on your end.

Paul reminds us to "live a life filled with love, following the example of Christ. He loved us and offered himself as a sacrifice for us, a pleasing aroma to God" (Ephesians 5:2).

Dignity, respect, honor—old fashioned traits that we can rely on to guide us through the end of a relationship. If we use these, we will live without regrets and know that we have handled our relationships as God has commanded.

The LORD grants wisdom! From his mouth come knowledge and understanding. He grants a treasure of common sense to the honest. He is a shield to those who walk with integrity. He guards the paths of the just and protects those who are faithful to him. Then you will understand what is right, just, and fair, and you will find the right way to go.

—PROVERBS 2:6-9

CONSIDER THIS

- Is there a way to break off a relationship so that you both can still grow into your fullest life?
- While there is never a perfect way to end a relationship, how would you want to be treated if a break was needed?
- Think about a time in your life when a relationship ended— an end that either you initiated or the other person did. What would you have done differently? What have you learned since then about ways to conduct yourself and ways to treat the other person?
- Is it possible that a lot of our heartache and relational chaos is simply the by-product of our stubborn refusal to place constraints on our moral behavior?

PUT IT INTO PRACTICE

Breaking Up No-No's

I used to think this was common sense, but I've heard so many stories of this happening, I want to bring it out in the open. Declaring or offering dignity to someone, especially in the midst of a breakup, means giving them the respect of doing it in person. No e-mail, no voice mail, no texting. Face-to-face.

If you've broken up with someone using one of these electronic media, please do the hard thing, the *right* thing, and go back and make it right. As uncomfortable as it is, ask to meet that person (this really goes for all conflict with friends, family, and others who are close to us), and present your issues in person.

The old fashioned way doesn't hide. It owns. It takes responsibility.

You can leave then, knowing you did the right thing.

setting your priorities

It's all icing, no cake. It's not enough. Commitment should come first, not the other way around.

—CLAY, *OLD FASHIONED*

MY MOTHER IS A CANNER. She takes the food my father grows in his garden and cans it, preparing for the winter. My grandmother was also a canner. And a saver. She lived during the Depression and understood the importance of thinking and preparing for whatever the future held.

The real Aunt Zella (the inspiration for the character in *Old Fashioned*) also grew up during the Depression and used to make a single paper napkin last a week—continuing to fold it over and over to the clean spot. She knew she needed to think about the future.

I've found that same ideal is important with respect to our goals. Who do you want to be? What do you want, and what are you looking for?

What are you going to do to move closer to those goals?

Bestselling author of *Blue Like Jazz* Donald Miller suggests that as we think about the vision of our future, we should view it from the perspective of a story or movie: "Have a vision for your life and let that vision guide you. If you want to have a family someday, then in your daily decisions think of your life as a movie. For example, in dating, ask yourself, 'Would this girl or this guy be a scene I'd want in the movie about a family someday?'"[1]

Obviously the most important goal to pursue is growing deeper in our faith. God wants us to pursue him with our life and our calling. The writer of Hebrews reminds us, "Let us strip off every weight that slows us down, especially the sin that so easily trips us up. And let us run with endurance the race God has set before us. We do this by keeping our eyes on Jesus, the champion who initiates and perfects our faith" (Hebrews 12:1-2).

Our faith needs to be the top priority, with everything else being viewed and considered through that lens. That means everything we do, say, and even think needs to stand against what our faith would have us do, say, and think.

Our vision and goals help shape our future, but they also shape who we will become. Donald Miller mentions that when he visits prisoners, he notices over and over they all have a common thread: they had no vision for their lives. "They lived in the moment," he says. "They reacted in the moment. They were unwilling to sacrifice for the sake of a longer narrative, and it got them into trouble."[2]

I'm not suggesting if you don't have a vision you're going to end up in jail! But a vision keeps us focused on the prize we want. Proverbs 29:18 tells us, "When people do not accept divine guidance, they run wild." The King James Version puts it this way: "Where there is no vision, the people perish."

Decide what you want and who you want to be, and let that guide how you live your life.

For example, Robert Pattinson is a popular actor. I've heard single Christian women who are committed to Christ talk on and on about how "hot" he looks and how awesome he is. What are they really saying? They're not saying Robert Pattinson is awesome because he's pursuing God with his life; they're sending the message that Robert Pattinson is awesome because he has charisma, a great body, and is handsome. It has nothing to do with who he is as a person.

We may not think there's anything wrong with appreciating what God created. But going back to the old fashioned way, if we're living a life of nobility and virtue, we're aware of how our words and actions affect others. So imagine that we're standing around and discussing Robert Pattinson and a young Christian man overhears the conversation. He's trying to live a godly life and to shape himself into the type of man who would make a good husband and father and neighbor and person. But he receives the message, *What you're doing isn't really as important as Robert Pattinson* (or whomever—fill in the blank). Or vice versa, for the men who ogle an attractive woman.

I would be remiss if somewhere in this book I didn't at least mention living together, or cohabiting ("shacking up," some used to say). A few years ago I was speaking about marriage to a roomful of Christian engaged couples. The pastor asked me to "share my wisdom" based on a book I'd written about the emotional side of being engaged and planning a wedding. In the middle of my talk with them, I asked a question and encouraged them to respond. While I don't remember the question I asked, I do remember that each couple—except one—responded with an answer that indicated they were living together. (That wasn't even the question!) Such confusing times. I watched the pastor through this interchange and noticed he had no issue with singles living together as husband and wife. I couldn't shake a feeling of despair after that.

On the surface, the idea of living together makes sense. It sounds good. But it can be so deeply damaging to a relationship. It makes it difficult to set up boundaries when there never were any before. It places a wall between you and God. And statistically speaking, the probability of divorce and/or abuse is far greater[3]. As you consider both who God calls you to be and what is best for your future marriage relationship, a clear vision and well-defined priorities will help you avoid the cultural snare of cohabiting before marriage.

Without a clear vision and set of priorities, we can easily forget the messages we send about ourselves. Don't allow yourself to fall into the trap of not having a clear direction for your life and what you want for your relationships. The clearer you are, the less chance you'll settle, the more likely you'll get great blessings, and ultimately, the more you'll turn into the person you really want to become.

> Whoever pursues righteousness and unfailing love will find life, righteousness, and honor.
>
> —PROVERBS 21:21

CONSIDER THIS

What else does the Bible say about pursuing positive goals?

- "Seek the Kingdom of God above all else, and live righteously, and he will give you everything you need." —Matthew 6:33
- "All athletes are disciplined in their training. They do it to win a prize that will fade away, but we do it for an eternal prize. So I run with purpose in every step. I am not just shadowboxing. I discipline my body like an athlete, training it to do what it should." —1 Corinthians 9:25-27
- "Pursue righteousness and a godly life, along with faith, love, perseverance, and gentleness." —1 Timothy 6:11
- "Run from anything that stimulates youthful lusts. Instead, pursue righteous living, faithfulness, love, and peace. Enjoy the companionship of those who call on the Lord with pure hearts." —2 Timothy 2:22

JOURNAL

- Take some time to write what you want out of life. Go deeper than the simple "I want a mate and a family." For each item you list, write why you want that and how it would affect your relationship with God.
- Who do you want to become? What character traits do you desire? Why? In what ways can you pursue those and make them a priority?
- Is God a priority in your life? Or is finding a mate? Does God set the priorities in your life?

waiting for my real life to begin

What are you afraid of? Let God act. Abandon yourself to Him. You will suffer, but you will suffer with love, peace, and consolation. . . . You will weep, but your tears will be sweet, and God Himself will come with satisfaction to dry them.

—FRANÇOIS FÉNELON

THE OTHER DAY I was at a coffee shop and overheard a woman on her cell phone mutter, "What's the use? I'm never going to get married."

I felt terrible for her, because I've been there. And maybe you have too.

The waiting can be so frustrating. And it can lead us to despair if we're not careful. It can also lead us to do things we wouldn't necessarily do—such as get involved with people we clearly know aren't right for us—because we wonder if the wait is really worth it and if what we do even matters at all.

It is worth it. It does matter. The key is that we have to keep our eyes focused on the big picture, not simply what we currently can or can't see.

When we look at our current situation, we can allow fear and anxiety to seep into our minds and attitudes: *I see no options. What if God wants me to be alone?*

We need to remember that part of God's plan for us *is* the wait. He's not saying, "Hang out here and wallow around until you can finally start your life."

No, he's behind the scenes working ("God causes everything to work together for the good of those who love God and are called according to his purpose for them," Romans 8:28). And he wants us to work as well. Part of that work is waiting. But a bigger part of the work is moving forward in pursuit of God's plans for us.

It's sort of like missing great community with your friends because you'd rather sit at home every Friday night waiting for the phone to ring from a special someone. (I know, that's a little extreme.)

It's the attitude, *I'm waiting for my* real *life to begin.*

Diana is in her thirties and still single. While she's "waiting," she bought a condo, started on her master's degree, writes a blog, took up an instrument, and travels. She's not halting her life. She's living her *real* life now.

I'm not going to tickle your ears with promises that if you do everything the old fashioned way, if you work at growing your character to become more Christlike, if you practice self-control in your actions and thoughts, then God will bless you with a spouse. You and I both know that isn't true. God may have plans for you that include a spouse. If so, great. God may have plans for you that call you to a life of being single. If so—*gulp*—great. Blessed be the name of the Lord either way. It isn't a punishment; it's simply a different road. And God promises to walk it with you the whole way.

Perhaps one way to look at it is to understand that we are called to be single until we are called to be married.[1]

William Booth, who founded the Salvation Army, said, "The greatness of a man's power is the measure of his surrender." Impatience gets us nowhere. But if we persist in trusting that God has a plan, if we take our time, and if we pray for divine help, then we have chosen the noble and good things to do.

Waiting, loneliness, fear—they are all opportunities to lean into God. I've been there. I know the argument you can make: "Sure, it's easy for you to lecture me on waiting. You're married. You've got your mate." Yes, you're right. My journey includes having a spouse. But I know the pain of God not granting my request. I've waited for a child, and none has come. God has chosen not to bless me in that way. And I've had to work through that waiting and longing and fear.

Both you and I, in our differing circumstances, are left with a choice. Do we trust God? Do we believe that he hasn't forgotten us? Do we know that he is working on our behalf and that he has a divine purpose for us—regardless of our marital or parenting status? If we say yes to any of those things, then we must *act* as though we believe it to the core of who we are.

God is with us! We can boldly approach him (see Hebrews 4:16) with our concerns. And he will hear us (see 1 John 5:14-15). The comfort we need will begin to flow into our souls. Thoughts will begin to flood our minds, all appropriate to the need at hand. Then we know our requests have been listened to and answered.

God is the epitome of nobility and virtue and chivalry!

When things aren't going our way and everywhere we turn seems to be a dead end and we make another mistake and we wonder when the loneliness will go away and we feel as though God has let us down and we are on the verge of giving up, God will show up. While we're waiting, if we're alert and looking for him, we will see his fingerprints all over our lives.

So don't give up. Don't allow despair to steal your freedom and joy. This life you are living *right now* is part of the bigger story of God's work. And you do matter to God. He has not—he will not— forget you or leave you hanging.

Don't get tired of doing what is good. Don't get discouraged and give up, for we will reap a harvest of blessing at the appropriate time.

—GALATIANS 6:9

CONSIDER THIS

Ponder these quotes and Scripture verses. Think about times in your life when they have proved true. Let them bring you comfort and help you gain a renewed sense of determination.

- "Let me ask you something. If someone prays for patience, you think God gives them patience? Or does he give them the opportunity to be patient? If he prayed for courage, does God give him courage, or does he give him opportunities to be courageous? If someone prayed for the family to be closer, do you think God zaps them with warm fuzzy feelings, or does he give them opportunities to love each other?" — God, *Evan Almighty*
- "Let us come boldly to the throne of our gracious God. There we will receive his mercy, and we will find grace to help us when we need it most." —Hebrews 4:16
- "Give all your worries and cares to God, for he cares about you." —1 Peter 5:7

part of a bigger story

I don't want to be a product of my environment. I want my environment to be a product of me.

—FRANK COSTELLO, *THE DEPARTED*

ONE OF MY FAVORITE television shows is *The Andy Griffith Show.* When Andy Griffith died, bloggers and journalists, conservatives and liberals, religious and atheists all found a common bond as they mourned: it felt like the passing of Mayberry, that old fashioned, idyllic place run by the easygoing sheriff. Mayberry was a place where everyone knew and cared for their neighbors, where life was slower and innocence was something to be celebrated, a place where love reigned supreme and mercy, patience, and wisdom were gifts to be freely offered.

What was so different about this particular place? And why do people long to live in Mayberry? Andy Griffith believed, "It was all about love."[1]

So many mourned the sheriff's passing and said, "We need more Mayberry."

"But if we no longer have Mayberry, whose fault is that?" a friend said recently. "We created the world we live in. We want the innocence of Mayberry, but not the responsibility or accountability or restriction. Mayberry only works when people look out for one another and adhere to some societal set of norms."

He's right. People want both *Fifty Shades of Grey* and Mayberry. They want the peace and serenity of Mayberry, but not the sacrifice or limits. They want Mayberry, but they still want Vegas.

That's one of the benefits of pursuing the old fashioned way: the true return of Mayberry and everything good that it stands for is possible. It's impossible to live the old fashioned way and *not* pass on its benefits. People watch our lives. And as we consistently live out the truth of what we believe to be good for us, others are offered the opportunity to test it for themselves.

In *Old Fashioned*, as Clay lives out his "theory" about men and women, his friends may poke fun or roll their eyes, but eventually, they begin to see for themselves that he may have grasped some truth that could work for them, too: a father turns off a radio program that his young daughter doesn't need to overhear; a cohabiting couple begin to understand the importance and sacredness of marriage and decide to wed.

The old fashioned way is not about us, ultimately. It's about honoring God and others. Our lives and the decisions we make about our relationships are part of a bigger story; we're all part of God's story. We are meant to pass along the traditions to the next generation. As we've learned, we in turn mentor others.

It's such a simple idea: *This is about something bigger than me, so I'm going to hold strong. No matter how silly or ridiculous it seems, I'm just going to do this.*

"I've seen that play out," Rik Swartzwelder, the creator of *Old Fashioned*, told me. "I haven't done this perfectly in my life. But every time I have honored that 'threshold' principle, I have never regretted it. And I've witnessed over and over again the beautiful change that can come by living the old fashioned way. But it took me hearing the stories and then seeing others trying to actually live it out to point me in a new direction. Thinking that way was so outside of my nature, I needed the living example. I think we all do."

A lot of ideas about being old fashioned are just acknowledging the reality of the world. This world is a battleground. The devil is a roaring lion. And being old fashioned isn't being negative or pessimistic. It's being realistic about the world and about our place in it. Not just about other people and not just about the world outside, but about the world in each of us. Our following the old fashioned way acknowledges that, is deadly serious about it. And in the light of this, we structure our lives accordingly. That's part of God's story for us.

Jesus looks at all of us, sees the best we can be, our potential. At the same time he's realistic about our struggles. He will never flinch or be surprised when we fall short. In a sense I think that's what being old fashioned is. It's being very realistic in our striving for something different and better and allowing God to use our good and our downfalls to mentor others.

Go home to your family, and tell them everything the Lord has done for you and how merciful he has been.

—MARK 5:19

CONSIDER THIS

Developing a Rhythm of Life

One of the books on Clay's bookshelf in the movie *Old Fashioned* is *The Rule of St. Benedict.* St. Benedict (ca. 480–547) is often called the founder of Western monasticism. His greatest accomplishment was his *Rule,* which considered setting aside our own wills to pursue complete obedience to Christ. It spells out the importance of structure and finding a rhythm of life to help facilitate our spiritual growth and maturity and help protect others from us and us from others.

As you consider setting up a structure and rhythm in your life, particularly with regard to your relationships, what would you include? What would you dismiss?

JOURNAL

Read these quotes, and write in your journal what they mean to you. Then describe some ways you can make them active in your life and interactions with others.

- "I don't want to be a product of my environment. I want my environment to be a product of me." —Frank Costello, *The Departed*
- "The greatness of a man's power is the measure of his surrender." —William Booth
- "Being old fashioned is now strangely countercultural. Mayberry has somehow become the new punk rock. It's outside the norm. It's different. So what? If God has placed a longing in your heart for a better way to live, who cares what the current batch of revolving-door cultural gatekeepers have to say about it? Be different." —Rik Swartzwelder

christ alone

Once I read [the Bible] for myself, I couldn't make fun of it anymore. Maybe someone else could, but I couldn't. I felt accountable for the first time in my life.

—CLAY, *OLD FASHIONED*

HAVE YOU EVER DONE SOMETHING you knew was wrong, and while you were doing it, a little voice inside you was yelling, *Don't do it. Don't do it! Make a different choice?*

Everyone is born with a conscience that gives us moral direction. And when we hit up against it, it goes off like a Mack truck backing up—*beep, beep, beep, beep.* The more we listen to it, the clearer it is, and we are rewarded with a clean slate, no regrets, and a joyful, light feeling. The more we ignore it, though, the quieter the beeping becomes. It never completely goes away, but it gets easier to disregard. And instead of being rewarded with a joyful, light feeling, we live with a heavier feeling. We can be happy, but not have inner peace and joy.

That disregard for the beeping can lead us into wrong choices and decisions, or what the old fashioned label called it: sin.

That word, *sin*, is an uncomfortable word that we've shied away from in our culture—and even in the church. Because we're so focused on being "politically correct" and "tolerant," we prefer to use words that don't make us feel bad about ourselves. So we call them *mistakes, hiccups, slipups, oversights, lacks of clarity, oopsies.*

A mistake doesn't sound so bad. It holds our action at a distance, so we aren't held accountable. We say things like "I lie, but I'm not a liar"; "I cheated on my spouse, but I'm not an adulterer"; "I talk about others behind their backs, but I'm not a gossip."

But here's the problem: a mistake is doing something we didn't realize at the time was wrong. (I mistakenly gave you a ten-dollar bill when I meant to give you a twenty.) It's usually caused by poor judgment, a lack of information, or a misunderstanding.

Sin, on the other hand, is definitely brought on by poor judgment, but it's knowing about something and then doing it anyway. It's an act of rebellion—against God, ourselves, and others.

Murdering someone is a sin because obviously it dishonors another person, clearly rebels against God and his will, and causes harm. And in Jesus' view, hating someone else is just as sinful as murder; thinking lustfully about another person is just as sinful as committing adultery. As we talked about before, the sin starts with our minds.

When we think about sin, we have to think about God's perfect standard. We were created by a holy God who cannot tolerate anything that goes against his perfection. And he calls us to be holy as well (see Leviticus 11:45; Matthew 5:48; Romans 12:2).

How can we possibly live above sin and be holy if we are broken?

Knowing our human nature and propensity toward immorality, God created a way for us to bridge the gap between his holiness and our sinfulness: Jesus. Jesus, who lived and died a perfect life, who conquered death and was raised to life—he became the payer of our sins. He took them upon himself so that we wouldn't have to pay the consequences of our sinfulness. The writer of Hebrews explains it this way: "Just think how much more the blood of Christ will purify our consciences from sinful deeds so that we can worship the living God. For by the power of the eternal Spirit, Christ offered himself to God as a perfect sacrifice for our sins" (Hebrews 9:14).

One thing the old fashioned way has never shied away from is calling sin *sin*. It recognizes our weaknesses and failures and calls them what they are. It isn't soft on morality but draws a line in the sand, saying, "You may not like it, it may make you feel uncomfortable, you may want to blur the lines, but there is a clear line here. And ignoring it or saying it isn't there doesn't make it disappear. It's there whether you believe it or not."

The world isn't a playground; it's a battleground. In my own life, and in the lives of many believers I know and love, we've gotten into trouble when we miss this essential fact of our reality. We have become almost too friendly with the world.

Being old fashioned gets back to clearly delineating black from white, day from night, wrong from right, and living that out in our lives. We do that by practicing daily righteousness, with the understanding that we obey God's will because it's our relational calling to do so. We strive to uphold God's holy, perfect standard (through Christ), and we model and stir in other people a vision of what love can look like.

Being old fashioned isn't supposed to pile on guilt—on ourselves or others. That was a weakness for Clay because he didn't fully grasp that holiness isn't pride or works based. Living a holy life is acknowledging every day, "God, I'm offering my life, my thoughts, my actions, my everything to you today and asking that, through the Holy Spirit's help, because of Jesus' sacrifice for me, you would shape me into your likeness. Give me the will and the strength to be obedient every moment of this day."

You do that every day. Sometimes every minute. And as you continue to offer your life, God slowly transforms you into his likeness.

You can change your behavior, but it doesn't draw you closer to God. It's not about rules; it's about offering yourself to God—that makes you *want* to live a holy life, not feel *obligated* to live it.

Calling our failings sin takes courage and humility. If we push away from this view and run from mess to mess, we will never grow. We will continue to make the same poor choices every time. And sooner or later, there will be nowhere left to run.

"If only it were all so simple," wrote Alexander Solzhenitsyn. "If only there were evil people somewhere insidiously committing evil deeds, and it were necessary only to separate them from the rest of us and destroy them. But the line dividing good and evil cuts through the heart of every human being. And who is willing to destroy a piece of his own heart?" Jesus tells us the way of holiness is a narrow and difficult path (see Matthew 7:14). Asking God to remold our soul requires that we put to death, over and over, our natural desires.

The apostle Paul encourages us to "work hard to show the results of your salvation, obeying God with deep reverence and fear" (Philippians 2:12).

Fortunately, we do not have to do that alone. Jesus is willing—no matter what we've done or had done to us—to walk with us on the journey of the old fashioned way.

Don't copy the behavior and customs of this world, but let God transform you into a new person by changing the way you think. Then you will learn to know God's will for you, which is good and pleasing and perfect.

—ROMANS 12:2

PUT IT INTO PRACTICE

Make It Real

When someone in my church makes a public profession that they
have turned away from living a life of sin to following Jesus and
living according to his model, they will write out their sins on a
piece of paper, then come forward and nail it to a wooden cross.
They are free, forgiven, no longer bound to the past. They are
signifying the truth of 2 Corinthians 5:17: "Anyone who belongs
to Christ has become a new person. The old life is gone; a new
life has begun!"

If you haven't gotten real about the sin in your life (and understand that everyone has sinned), why not do it now? It isn't a
magic formula—it's just getting honest with God and confessing
that you've rebelled against him. You've gone your own way and it
hasn't worked, and now you want him to forgive you through the
sacrifice Jesus made and to lead your life. It's that simple.

CONSIDER THIS

Still Not Convinced?

Still not completely comfortable with the whole idea of sin and
how serious it is to God? Go to BibleGateway.com and type in
the word *holy*. Read the Scripture passages that come up, and
contemplate who God really is and what that means for the
decisions you make in your life.

by god's grace

You are loved. You are so loved. Oh, my child. You are. We never fully arrive this side of heaven.

—AUNT ZELLA, *OLD FASHIONED*

THE PREVIOUS READING WAS A TOUGHIE, HUH? No one likes to have someone tell them, "Hey, you're a sinner." Fortunately, we have a God who doesn't stop there. He holds his arms wide open and says, "I have forgiven you, and I don't hold that sin against you. I love you. I love you. I love you."

Think about that. A holy God. An imperfect person. And a love that bridges the chasm.

I can know God loves me, but sometimes it's a mental knowledge without being a heart understanding. When I meditate on how much the God of the universe loves *me*, knows *me*, cares about *me*, I become emotionally overwhelmed. I cannot fully comprehend it. Paul says,

> Christ will make his home in your hearts as you trust in
> him. Your roots will grow down into God's love and keep

you strong. And may you have the power to understand, as all God's people should, how wide, how long, how high, and how deep his love is. May you experience the love of Christ, though it is too great to understand fully. Then you will be made complete with all the fullness of life and power that comes from God. (Ephesians 3:17-19)

Even Paul knew we couldn't completely grasp how amazing God's love is.

We are all made of the same stuff. If we think we are safe from making the mistakes of others, we are kidding ourselves. There but for the grace of God go any of us.

Think about the reality shows that go into communities, find people who are deserving of some type of kindness, and then make that a reality (*Extreme Makeover: Home Edition*, *Three Wishes*). They're such great stories to watch. A key component of each story is that someone is deserving of that kindness, right?

But what if you went into a community and found people who weren't deserving and you gave to them? Isn't that the gospel?

We're not being slack on sin. There are people who exploit and deceive other people. Not everyone is good at heart. But I've seen what true grace can do to people, and it is genuinely amazing.

The gospel isn't that you deserve something and goodness comes to you. The gospel is the truth that we deserve nothing and in spite of that God offers grace.

This is what Clay and Amber discover in *Old Fashioned*. And while theirs is a fictionalized story, there is nothing fictional about the truth of receiving that kind of grace. We can tap into something that is close to the heart of God.

I can look at so many things in my life that have made me undeserving of grace that I realize if it weren't for unmerited, undeserved mercy, I would be hopeless. God loves us despite what is unlovely in us. But in his old fashioned goodness, he doesn't leave us there, unchanged. And he doesn't wait for us to be good enough to deserve his forgiveness before he offers it.

Singer/songwriter Leonard Cohen (known for songs such as "Hallelujah") said, "There is a crack in everything; that's how the light gets in." Only God can fulfill us completely, and only as we are completed by him are we prepared and ready to love another person in a healthy and redemptive way.

As you take this journey going back to the good qualities of tradition and old fashioned character traits, I encourage you to focus not so much on finding the right person romantically, but instead on committing (or recommitting) your life to God and opening yourself to his purposes for you. Love isn't a romantic ideal. It is pure and holy and active. It doesn't rely on our feelings but on God's truth. Remember, as Paul said, "Three things will last forever—faith, hope, and love—and the greatest of these is love" (1 Corinthians 13:13).

Old fashioned isn't a label to be avoided. Old can be new again. Old fashioned can become an insurrection, a cultural revolution. And it needs only to start with one voice. Will you be that voice?

> Sin is no longer your master, for you no longer live under
> the requirements of the law. Instead, you live under the
> freedom of God's grace.
>
> —ROMANS 6:14

CONSIDER THIS

The old fashioned way fully acknowledges just how difficult it is to live life as a single person. Jesus knew this way of life very well. The writer of Hebrews reminds us, "This High Priest of ours understands our weaknesses, for *he faced all of the same testings we do*, yet he did not sin" (Hebrews 4:15, emphasis added).

Jesus knew what it was like to feel all alone. He knew how long a night could be; he knew the feeling of just wanting to be held, to be connected, to be loved. The Creator of the universe knew and knows exactly how you feel. Exactly.

JOURNAL

Many years ago, a friend gave me a blessings journal so that every day I could list the ways God showed up in my life that day and offered his love, direction, and grace. I would encourage you to start your own blessings journal to remember God's goodness to you. Then every day you can write the ways God has blessed you.

satisfaction guaranteed!

I HOPE THIS BOOK has given you the encouragement you need to pursue old fashioned ideals and ways of living.

I remember being single and being really sensitive about the "promise": that if I do everything right and live honorably, then I'll be guaranteed a wonderful life with a fabulous spouse, a brood of kids, a white picket fence around my *House Beautiful* minimansion, and vacations at Disneyland Paris (romantic Paris *and* Disney? Can anything be better?). All my dreams would come true.

We know better, don't we? But still. It can be easy to equate "righteous" living with winning the lottery. Even some churches fall victim to this mentality. A lot of churches and Christians shun the idea of the prosperity gospel—except with the idea of being single.

If you just pray enough . . .

If you just keep your virginity . . . or "born again" virginity . . .

If you do everything on this checklist . . .

It seeps even into Christian thinking.

There's an implied prosperity gospel prevalent in our experience in the evangelical church (not health and wealth). If you are a good Christian, then you will be rewarded with a mate and a family.

Ultimately, it really isn't about whether or not you get a spouse (although I know that's difficult to hear). It's about being a living argument against the status quo.

So let's talk about applying old fashioned principles to our living and loving.

I can say with 100 percent confidence that when I practice this way of living, I have peace and calmness within me. I have no regrets, and my relationships are stronger and more authentic. I'm a more loving and gentle person.

But I can also say with 100 percent certainty that following old fashioned principles will not guarantee you a mate—no matter how much your church's small group may say otherwise.

Even if you do all these things, that doesn't necessarily mean you'll get the mate of your dreams. But if you live this way, your life will become so honoring to God that it will *become* the life of your dreams.

Not everyone's story is the same, and God works in all kinds of ways. We're all part of God's story. Ultimately it's not our story, although we play a big role. It may end up that a purpose of your life may be part of God's story in which, by living the life that God has laid before you, you're paving the way for someone you may not even know.

So here's the old fashioned guarantee: there are no guarantees— except for one (and it's a satisfaction guarantee). If you commit to living out God's purposes for your life right now, right where you are, and not waiting for romantic love to "find you," you will build a strong foundation for your life to be rich and fulfilling. And it will grow in you a confidence to accept who you are—and who you are meant to be. You don't have to settle for the old ways of relationships.

God's love has already found you! Soaking in that love will inspire within you a longing for a new kind of romance and love—the old fashioned kind. And you will never regret those old fashioned choices.

acknowledgments

Ginger Kolbaba would like to thank . . .

Rik Swartzwelder: You're a delight, a hoot, a passionate man of God, and a great writer, director, and actor. Thank you for allowing me to shamelessly squeeze my way into this project.

Carol Traver: I adore you. Thank you for your belief in me with this project. I appreciate your sense of humor, your professionalism, and your love of Mexican food. Front Street Cantina soon?

Jonathan Schindler: What a great editor you are. Your insights have been invaluable. I've so enjoyed working with you! And that you can sing Styx songs is icing on the cake. Thank you.

Nathan Nazario: Thanks for your thumbs-up on my work. Much as I tried, I was unable to get the word *heathen* into the manuscript. I hope you'll forgive me for that. (See Day 40 if you're having trouble with the forgiveness stuff.)

The excellent folks at Tyndale: You rock. You rock. You rock. Thanks for letting me be part of your team on this and so many other projects.

You truly have a heart for God that shows in the work you do and the products you produce.

My parents, John and Genny McFarland: Thank you for instilling old fashioned principles in me and modeling that they can be cool. And yes, Mom, thank you for telling me what *not* to wear.

My mother-in-law, Ruth Kolbaba: Thank you for allowing me to rudely type away on my computer while visiting you in the hospital every day. I'm glad you're now cancer free and on the road to recovery. God's fingerprints are all over you!

My sweet Scott: I didn't realize how old fashioned you are until I started to work on this project. And it's made me love you even more. Thanks for putting up with me—oh, all the time.

My gentle, gracious God: I'm at a loss for words that could express how amazing you are. My heart, my mind, my soul. Take them all. They are yours.

Rik Swartzwelder's acknowledgments:

If you had told my friends and me when we were all in high school that I would ever have anything to do with a book like this, we would have laughed in your face. God has such a sense of humor. . . .

Thanks to all of the people and churches along the way that helped nurture a cynical and mocking heart into one with room and respect for the Creator. This book would have never existed without you, the faithful (and even unfaithful) parishioners of Broadway United Methodist Church (New Philadelphia, Ohio), First Baptist Church (New Philadelphia), St. Wendelin Catholic Parish & High School (Fostoria, Ohio), Lake Gibson Church of the Nazarene (Lakeland, Florida), Sligo Seventh-Day Adventist Church (Takoma Park, Maryland), Bayshore Mennonite Church (Sarasota, Florida), First Lutheran Church (Burbank, California), St. Robert Bellarmie Catholic Church (Burbank), and especially my small groups from Damascus Road Community Church (Mt. Airy, Maryland) and Trinity Presbyterian Church (Lakeland).

Specifically, I need to thank Pastors Richard Fredericks and Tim Rice for teaching me so much about God's grace and living with transparency and accountability in the context of a loving and compassionate community.

For being spiritual guideposts for me at points along the way, I am indebted to Jack and Bonnie Eickhoff, John Lindberg, Vester Gravley, Mark Feldbush, Will Woodrow, Jerry and Michelle Rader, David and Renee Michael, Bret Mooney (and family), Greg Cumbaa, and a special nod to Shawn and Melissa Sulzener (I *still* have the postcard you sent me tucked in my Bible—Proverbs 3:5-6).

Tony Campolo, thanks again for giving me permission to adapt your *Agnes Story* into my short film *The Least of These*. You inspired me to dream big, and it made all the difference.

Ginger Kolbaba, you are amazing! You wove together our conversations and ideas in a way that so exceeded my expectations. I simply can't thank you enough, but I will keep trying! Yes, I am using exclamation points!

Carol Traver, Jonathan Schindler, and the whole Tyndale team, thank you for having a vision that was even broader and more far reaching than I ever imagined when working on the screenplay and film. Your passion, talent, and humor are both a pleasure and a wonderful example to this publishing novice.

Bill Reeves and the Working Title Agency, thank you for navigating these waters with such wisdom and grace. You are a blessing.

Phillip Sherwood, you kept the dream and the spirit alive—thank you. Zach Gray, David George, and Randy Craven, thanks to all of you for providing the creative space and support needed for us to cross the finish line and turn dreams into reality.

For not giving up on me (or anyone else) and for giving us all the opportunity to be a part of *your* love story, Father God, thank you.

And finally, there are just a few names I'd really like to mention here (but for the sake of privacy will not), names of beautiful souls that did much to show me the reality of God's overwhelming love and also the joys and elegant anguish that can exist only when two human hearts become vulnerable to one another . . . and fumble toward loving each other the same way God loves, with gentleness, truth, and mercy.

There is indeed *Hope for the Flowers*. . . .

I will never forget.

Thank you.

getting started

If you've read through the forty days and think, *Okay, you've sold me on trying this—but how do I start?* read on.

One thing I've tried to do is not lay out specifics that suggest if you just do x, y, and z, exactly that way, then you're set. What works for one person may not work for another. One person may need tighter boundaries, such as never being alone with a member of the opposite sex or never holding hands or kissing until the wedding day. You may not need those particular boundaries.

Really, only you and God—within the context of a loving, supportive, and truthful community—should determine where your boundaries are. Deep down in your gut, if you truly listen to God's leading, you'll know what you need to do. He gave us the great Counselor, the Holy Spirit, to help us with those determinations. And if you ask, trust me—the Holy Spirit will answer.

But let's say you just need help getting started.

The first thing I'd encourage you to do is to practice some spiritual disciplines, such as praying, meditating on Scripture, and contemplation. Ultimately, living the old fashioned way isn't simply to snag a mate but to make *you* a strong potential mate—which means doing some soul care and building a solid character. Start by asking God to give you wisdom and discernment in your daily decisions, actions, conversations, and thoughts. And then set aside some time just to listen for God to talk to you.

I highly doubt it will be an audible "Hey you, this is God . . ." experience. Usually God speaks in whispered tones into our minds and hearts. Often he'll speak to us through the infallible Scriptures. If you hear him say something to you, test it against what the Bible says. If the two align, then you're good. If they don't, then throw that thought away.

The thing I've found with God is that when I ask for something, he usually doesn't give it to me directly but rather presents an opportunity for growth. In other words, if I ask God to help me be respectful toward others, he usually sends a really cranky person my way as an opportunity to practice and grow respect within me. You've been warned.

The same is true with getting started living the old fashioned way. As you ask God to help you live in a way that's pleasing to him, he'll provide opportunities for you to practice it. But the great thing is that he doesn't expect you to live that way on your own. He'll always be there to help, guide, and strengthen you.

So how do you get started?

First—and always!—pray for God to lead you, shape you, and strengthen you. Then watch as the opportunities start coming your way.

Spend time reading the Bible, focusing on and discovering who Jesus is and then emulating him.

Want more specifics? Check out my . . .

Ten Commandments for the Old Fashioned Way

1. Thou shalt not stay out after eleven with a person of the opposite sex, for nothing good happens. Thou shalt also be aware and careful of how much alone time you spend with a member of the opposite sex, for nothing

good comes from that temptation, either. It's a conscious choice. You are, in advance, making a choice about what will happen.

2. Thou shalt actively listen to the other person and give him or her thy full attention. For much is said when nothing is said. And much is said when everything is said—but only if you listen without trying to rush into getting your own opinions across. Everyone wants to be heard. Thou shalt always attempt to hear.

3. Thou shalt keep a check on thine emotions. Don't give them away any time, any place, to anyone. Do not rush into giving away your emotions, for once they are "all in," there is little hope to control them in a healthy way. Nor shalt thou overanalyze every single thing another person says or does to figure out some deeper meaning. Nor shalt thou overspiritualize: "God put it on my heart that you are the one for me." If God put it on your heart, he is big enough to put it on the other person's heart as well.

4. Thou shalt set ground rules up front, for both parties must be on the same page or thou willst fall prey to temptation. Thou shalt not try to set ground rules in a bedroom in the middle of a make-out session. Thou shalt also not try to set together time in the middle of the Super Bowl, when one party wants to have deep, meaningful conversation and the other wants to actually just watch the game.

5. Thou shalt not use "I love you" like air freshener. Words matter. Don't say things you don't mean.

6. Thou shalt hold the door for another. Look for ways to serve the other person. Are you looking for ways to serve or just what you can get from the other person? Treat the other person with respect and dignity. Every woman is someone's daughter. And every woman is a daughter of God. Every

man is someone's son. And every man is a son of God.
Think about that in terms of how you treat the other.

7. Thou shalt not waste anyone's time, including thine own.
Are you ready? Are you in a place where you bring something
healthy to another person? Or do you need to take a season
to ready yourself? Along these same lines, thou shalt lighten
up. Don't be so desperate. The Lord's timing is perfect but
can be frustratingly long and slow for us. Use the time well,
preparing yourself, getting to know and become comfortable
with yourself. Work at truly respecting yourself, using the gifts
God gave you, and appreciating the treasure you are as God's
special creation, made for a special purpose. Thou shalt not
settle just because you want a date on Friday night or because
everyone is hooking up or getting married. Thou shalt avoid
comparing thy situation with someone else's—in particular if
that someone else makes you frustrated, sad, jealous.

8. Thou shalt be ready to be considered different. Embrace
that. Old fashioned is like the eighties punk-rock scene.
Embrace it boldly and without apology. You owe no reason
or explanation to anyone else—you are living in light of
God's choices for you, and that is enough.

9. Thou shalt remember that thine old fashioned way is not a
set of rules that other people must follow. Don't turn your
old fashioned way into the world's. You can pursue it with
diversity and still be on the same path, moving in the same
direction. Continue to seek God's direction for *your* path.

10. Thou shalt pay attention to the original Ten Commandments
(see Exodus 20). They're much better than mine. Follow
the actual ten and the other two (see Matthew 22:36-40).
Remember, this world is a battleground, not a playground.
Pay attention. If you fail to plan, you plan to fail. And thou
shalt make a habit of inviting God into your choices.

conversation starters

You can find countless online links to personality profiles, couples' discussion guides, and a number of other questionnaires for yourself and your potential beloved. As you research those, I'd encourage you always to ask yourself if the approach of each particular resource leans toward an "I" and "Thou" relational understanding. Does it encourage you to work toward putting the other person first? Is it directing you to serve yourself or to love the other person?

To get you started, here are some questions for you and your significant other that I think are important to know the answers to. See where your answers overlap in your beliefs and where they don't, and talk about that.

Relational/Marital Expectations
- What do you think marriage is going to be?
- How would you define the perfect marriage?
- Do you know anyone who models that?
- Are there any absolute no-no's in a relationship?

Spirituality
- How do you view God?
- How often do your spiritual beliefs play a role in your decisions? Should they?

- Does church attendance matter?
- How involved in a church or a Bible study group should a couple be?
- Do you feel it's important to attend church together?
- Do you feel it's important to study the Bible and/or pray together? If so, what would that look like?
- What are your views on forgiveness?
- How would you respond to this statement: "This world is a battleground." What do you think that means? Do you agree? If you agree, how does it affect your life, your decisions, and your relationships?

Role Expectations

- How do you want to define your roles within the home?
- How would you view the balance of housekeeping duties?
- What house rules do you want in place? (For example: no guests after a certain hour; shoes on in the house or not.)

Finances

- How do you spend money?
- Would you consider yourself a saver or a spender? How would others define you?
- How much should you be able to spend without the other person knowing?
- What is your ideal standard of living? How close to that are you living now?
- What are your views on carrying debt?
- What kind of debt do you now have? What plans do you have to get debt free?
- What are your views on tithing or charitable giving? Should it be with every paycheck or on special occasions only?
- Who will handle the bill paying? Should it be done together?

Career

- What role does career play in your life? Do you see it as a vocation or as a job?
- After marriage, do you see that career continuing?
- Do you have aspirations for a different career? If so, what steps have you taken (or would you like to take) to make that career a reality?
- How does marriage play into your career? (For example, will you work shorter hours after marriage? Would you relocate?)
- What roles did career play in your family?
- After kids arrive, what role will career play then?
- Would you expect to continue working or stay at home with the kids?

Play Time

- How often do you take vacations?
- How often would you expect to take a vacation in marriage?
- How do you want to spend your days off?
- Where is your ideal vacation spot?
- How would you consider compromise in vacation?

Sexual History[1]

- What are your views on sex?
- In your family, was sex considered healthy and beautiful or a topic to be avoided?
- What expectations would you have about a sexual relationship within marriage?
- How often would you expect to have sex?
- Who should be the initiator?
- Have you ever had any unwanted sexual experiences or touch?

Children

- Do you want kids?

- How many children would you ideally like to have?
- If biological children are not a possibility for you, would you consider adoption?
- What are your views on discipline?

Communication
- How high do you rate integrity in communication?
- How much value do you place on the words you say?
- How do you view honesty? Are secrets ever okay? What about white lies?
- What is communication like in your family?
- How did your family disagree? Do you view that as a healthy way to argue?
- How would you like to handle disagreements in marriage?

Politics
- What are your political views? Are those views shared by your family, or have you come to them as an adult?
- How do you feel about voting and/or being politically active?
- How do you feel about those who don't share your views?
- What are your views on abortion? The death penalty? Taxes? Big government versus smaller government?
- How do you feel about owning a gun?

Friendship
- Are opposite-sex friendships okay after marriage?
- How involved with your friends do you anticipate being after you're married?
- Is it okay to have girls-only/guys-only weekends?

Culture/Hot Topics
- Is alcohol use okay? When is it not okay?
- How do you feel about using profanity? Are there particular words that you're completely uncomfortable using?

- How much television do you watch?
- What are your views on entertainment?
- Have you ever walked out of a movie? Why?
- What are your views on justice?
- What are your views on compassion?
- If somebody on the street asks you for money, what do you do?
- Have you ever hit anyone? If so, what were the circumstances?

Family/In-laws
- What was your house like growing up? Was it a safe place or a place filled with tension or chaos?
- What do you like about your family?
- What do you not like about your family—or wish were different?
- What expectations do you have about in-law relationships after marriage?
- How should holidays be split up?

Personality Distinctives
- Are you comfortable or uncomfortable with silence?
- How would you rate yourself as a listener?
- Are you an introvert (someone who gains energy by being alone or away from people) or an extrovert (someone who thrives on being around people)?
- Do you hold grudges, or are you able to let things go?
- What are your views on privacy in marriage?
- How strongly do you feel a need to have your own time versus being together all the time?
- In what pursuits do you find your greatest joy?
- What kind of humor do you like?
- Where's the line between okay humor and inappropriate humor?

Relationship Endings

- What are your views on divorce? Separation? Marriage counseling?
- Would you ever seek marital counseling? Why or why not?
- Do you know someone who has experienced a divorce? What effect has that had on you and your views of marriage?
- What are your plans to safeguard your marriage from adultery—both physical and emotional?

more resources

If you want to do a bit more reading on how best to spend this season of your life, check out these resources:

Chapman, Gary D. *The Five Love Languages*. Chicago: Northfield Publishing, 1992.

————. *The Five Love Languages: Singles Edition*. Chicago: Northfield Publishing, 2009.

Cloud, Henry and John Townsend. *Boundaries in Dating*. Grand Rapids, MI: Zondervan Publishing House, 2000.

Courtney, Camerin. *Table for One*. Grand Rapids, MI: Revell Publishing, 2002.

Courtney, Camerin and Todd Hertz. *The Unguide to Dating*. Grand Rapids, MI: Revell Publishing, 2006.

Elliot, Elisabeth. *Passion and Purity*. Grand Rapids, MI: Revell Publishing, 1984

Harris, Joshua. *I Kissed Dating Goodbye*. Colorado Springs: Multnomah Books, 2003.

————. *Boy Meets Girl*. Colorado Springs: Multnomah Books, 2005.

Ludy, Eric and Leslie. *When God Writes Your Love Story*. Colorado Springs: Multnomah Books, 2009.

Mullins, Rich and Ben Pearson. *The World as I Remember It*. Colorado Springs: Multnomah Books, 2004.

Nouwen, Henri J. M. *Life of the Beloved*. New York: The Crossroad Publishing Company, 2002.

Parrott, Les and Leslie. *Saving Your Marriage before It Starts*. Grand Rapids, MI: Zondervan Publishing House, 2006.

————. *Dot.com Dating*. Carol Stream, IL: Tyndale House Publishers, 2011.

Thomas, Gary. *The Sacred Search: A Couples' Conversation Guide*. Colorado Springs: David C. Cook Publishers, 2013.

a plot summary
of *Old Fashioned*

Old Fashioned (the movie and the book) focuses on Clay Walsh, a former frat boy in his midthirties who gives up his reckless carousing and now runs an antique shop in a small midwestern town. There he has become notorious for his lofty and outdated theories on love and romance.

When Amber Hewson, a free-spirited young woman with a wandering soul, drifts into the area and rents the apartment above his shop, she finds herself surprisingly drawn to his noble ideas, which are new and intriguing to her. And Clay, though he tries to deny and fight it, finds himself unable to resist being attracted to her spontaneous and passionate embrace of life. Through the course of the story, Clay must step out from behind his relational theories and Amber must overcome her fears and deep wounds as the two of them, together, attempt the impossible: an "old fashioned" courtship in contemporary America.

You may think Clay seems a little strange, awkward, and removed with his noble aspirations about romantic love. He is. Yet the fight he has had to fight to reclaim his virtue couldn't help but push him in the direction he went. You could say that, in a sense, Amber represents grace and Clay represents the law. Clay is all about the rules, the boundaries, the don'ts. Amber is all about joy, experience, the dos.

Their story explores how much they need each other—not just Clay and Amber but also law and grace. Both are needed for balance; both matter.

Ultimately, *Old Fashioned* reminds us that when we start to feel that how we live out our romantic lives doesn't matter all that much—that how we conduct ourselves and how we allow our relationships to progress doesn't matter—it does. It does matter. All of it matters.

endnotes

DAY 1. WHAT'S RIGHT ABOUT TODAY'S DATING SCENE

1. Quote taken from "This Is How We Met: Todd Hertz's story," *Hopeful Leigh*, http://www.leighkramer.com/blog/2012/04/this-is-how-we-met-todd-hertzs-story.html.

DAY 2. WHAT'S RIGHT ABOUT YESTERYEAR'S DATING SCENE

1. David Popenoe and Barbara Dafoe Whitehead, "Should We Live Together? What Young Adults Need to Know about Cohabitation before Marriage: A Comprehensive Review of Recent Research," *The Journal of Family Psychology*, 2009. http://www.smartmarriages.com/cohabit.html.
2. http://www.eightcitiesmap.com/transcript_bc.htm.

DAY 4. BUT I'VE DONE EVERYTHING RIGHT!

1. For example, see Proverbs 21:4; Habakkuk 2:4; Galatians 6:3; James 4:6.

DAY 7. WHAT DO YOU WANT?

1. Galatians 5:22-23.

DAY 9. RESPECT YOURSELF

1. Camerin Courtney and Todd Hertz, *The Unguide to Dating* (Grand Rapids, MI: Revell, 2006), number 11.

DAY 12. WHY BOUNDARIES MATTER

1. Elisabeth Elliot, *Passion and Purity: Learning to Bring Your Love Life under Christ's Control* (Grand Rapids, MI: Revell, 2002), 129.

DAY 13. EMOTIONAL PROMISCUITY

1. "Is There Such a Thing as Emotional Promiscuity?" Lies Young Women Believe blog. Interview with Brienne Murk by Erin Davis. http://www.liesyoungwomenbelieve.com /index.php?id=197.

DAY 15. *CAN* MEN AND WOMEN BE JUST FRIENDS?

1. The findings were published in the *Journal of Social and Personal Relationships*. http://spr.sagepub.com/content/early/2012/04/24/0265407512443611.abstract.
2. "Men, Women Can Be Friends, but Should They?" by Misty Harris, *Postmedia News*, May 4, 2012. http://www.canada.com/life/women+friends+should+they/6553963/story.html.

DAY 17. GOODNESS GRACIOUS
1. John W. Ritenbaugh, "The Fruit of the Spirit: Goodness." *Forerunner*, "Personal," August 1998. http://www.bibletools.org/index.cfm/fuseaction/Library.sr/CT/PERSONAL/k/251 /The-Fruit-of-Spirit-Goodness.htm.

DAY 20. CHASTITY. REALLY?
1. http://www.cdc.gov/nchs/data/nhsr/nhsr036.pdf.
2. Arlene Spenceley, "Why, at 26, She's Okay with Saving Sex for Marriage," *Chicago Sun-Times*, August 7, 2012. Accessed at http://www.suntimes.com/lifestyles/easy/14160916-423 /why-at-26-shes-ok-with-saving-sex-for-marriage.html.

DAY 21. THE PLEASURE OF PURITY
1. "*Fifty Shades of Grey* Phenomenon Is Taking Over," *Daily Herald*, August 19, 2012. http://m.dailyherald.com/dailyherald/db_32321/contentdetail.htm?contentguid=5ai8HI3g &full=true#display.
2. Ironically, a Methodist group purchased the Damson Dene Hotel ten years ago. The owner, Jonathan Denby, decided to make the switch because he thought it "inappropriate to distribute Bibles in today's secular society." From "*Fifty Shades of Grey* Replaces Bible at England's Damson Dene Hotel," *Huffington Post*, July 24, 2012. http://www.huffingtonpost.com/2012/07/24/fifty-shades-of-grey-replaces-bible _n_1699665.html.
3. "The Takeover of the Female Fantasy: Fifty Shades of Grey" by Ashley Moore. Kyria.com, May 29, 2012. http://blog.kyria.com/2012/05/the_takeover_of_the_female_fan.html.
4. I was the editor of *Marriage Partnership* magazine for more than ten years. In those years I received hundreds of letters from spouses who struggled with the issue of purity in their marriages.

DAY 22. A MODEST LONGING
1. "Debunking the 'Homewrecker' Myth after Kristen Stewart's Affair," by Halee Gray Scott. Her.meneutics blog, posted August 15, 2012. http://blog.christianitytoday.com /women/2012/08/debunking-the-homewrecker-myth.html?utm_source=%5blist .name%5d&utm_medium=Newsletter&utm_term=%5bmemberid%5d&utm _content=%5boutmail.messageid%5d&utm_campaign=2012.

DAY 23. THAT'S WHAT FRIENDS ARE FOR
1. http://pamphlets.quaker.org/phd/php264_jr.html.

DAY 24. ON ACCOUNTABILITY
1. If you have never seen *Gone with the Wind*, I highly recommend it. For the purposes of this illustration, I'll whittle the synopsis to this small portion: Scarlett O'Hara has a crush on Ashley Wilkes, who is married to Melanie. But Scarlett doesn't care and pursues him like a hussy throughout the movie. Ashley entertains her crush until finally toward the end of the movie, when he realizes the emotional entanglement he's allowed them both to get into, he puts a stop to it. Too little, too late, in my humble opinion.
2. "Debunking the 'Homewrecker' Myth after Kristen Stewart's Affair," by Halee Gray Scott. Her.meneutics blog. August 15, 2012. http://blog.christianitytoday.com/women/2012/08 /debunking-the-homewrecker-myth.html.

DAY 29. IN SEARCH OF THE PERFECT PERSON

1. Based on Romans 3:10.

DAY 30. I THINK I LOVE YOU

1. "Sometimes love has to drive the nail into its own hand" from "Sometimes Love" written by Chris Rice. © 1995 Clumsy Fly Music (admin. by Word Music, Inc.)/ASCAP. Second half of quote taken from liner notes for "Sometimes Love." Short Term Memories album, © 2004, Rocketown Records.

2. Kudos and thanks to Mike Breaux, pastor of Heartland Community Church in Rockford, Illinois, for presenting this self-evaluation during one of his messages at Willow Creek Community Church in South Barrington, Illinois.

DAY 31. A WORD TO THE MEN

1. "Why Young Men Aren't Manning Up," by Jonathan Sprowl. Today's Christian Woman blog. Posted January 24, 2012, http://blog.todayschristianwoman.com/2012/01 /why_young_men_arent_manning_up.html.

DAY 32. A WORD TO THE WOMEN

1. See Matthew 11:29; 21:5; 2 Corinthians 10:1, KJV.

2. "Why Young Men Aren't Manning Up," by Jonathan Sprowl. Today's Christian Woman blog. Posted January 24, 2012, http://blog.todayschristianwoman.com/2012/01 /why_young_men_arent_manning_up.html

DAY 36. SETTING YOUR PRIORITIES

1. "Why Donald Miller Thinks Life Should Be Hard." Interview by Ashley Moore. Today's Christian Woman blog. Posted April 10, 2012. http://blog.todayschristianwoman.com /2012/04/why_donald_miller_thinks_life.html.

2. Ibid.

3. See, for example, "The Timing of Cohabitation and Engagement: Impact on First and Second Marriages," *Journal of Marriage and the Family* 72, no. 4 (August 2010): 906–918. http://www.ncbi.nlm.nih.gov/pmc/articles/PMC2904561/.

DAY 37. WAITING FOR MY REAL LIFE TO BEGIN

1. My thanks to Rich Mullins for this idea.

DAY 38. PART OF A BIGGER STORY

1. "Andy Griffith: 'It Was All about the Love'" by Frank Smith. *Christianity Today*. July 4, 2012. http://www.christianitytoday.com/ct/2012/julyweb-only/andy-griffith.html.

APPENDIX B: CONVERSATION STARTERS

1. When you have this discussion, I would strongly urge you not to do it in private. There's nothing that says temptation more than talking about sex.